Leading for Change

A Renewed Focus on Teaching and Learning

E. Nola A

DETSELIG
ENTERPRISES LTD

Leading for Change

National Library of Canada Cataloguing in Publication Data

Aitken, A. J. (Arthur John)

Leading for change: a renewed focus on teaching and learning/ A.J. Aitken and E.N. Aitken

Includes bibliographic references.
ISBN 1-55059-255-6

1. Educational change. 2. Educational leadership. 3. Educational evaluation. 4. School management and organization. I. Aitken, E. Nola. II. Title.

LB2805.A37   2003   371.2   C2003-910489-3

DETSELIG
ENTERPRISES LTD

210-1220 Kensington Rd. N.W., Calgary, Alberta, T2N 3P5, Canada

Phone: (403) 283-0900/Fax: (403) 283-6947

E-mail: temeron@telusplanet.net

www.temerondetselig.com

We acknowledge the financial support of the Government of Canada through the Book Industry Development Program (BPIDP) for our publishing activities.

We also acknowledge the support of the Alberta Foundation for the Arts for our publishing program.

COMMITTED TO THE DEVELOPMENT OF CULTURE AND THE ARTS

ISBN 1-55059-255-6
SAN 115-0324
Printed in Canada

Contents

Acknowledgements 5

Introduction 7
   Purpose 7
   Who is this book for? 7

Preface 9
   The audience 9
   The knowledge base 9
   Structure of the chapters 10
   Chapter descriptions 10

About the Authors 13

Chapter One:
Introduction: Setting the Stage 15
   Stormy seas: The foundations for rebuilding .15
   Taking up the challenge 15
   First order of business: Restoring order 16
   How well are we informed? 17
   A leader's strategy 17
   Open communication and accountability . . .18
   An action plan 18
   Others' agendas, problems, wrinkles,
   and kinks 18
   Assessing progress and a perception check . . .19
   Another challenge: Implementing site-based
   decision-making 19

So far, what had been accomplished? 19
Workshop Questions 21

Chapter Two:
Establishing Structures for Community
and Learning Organization 23
   Community – without a purpose? 23
   Current practice – A paucity of introspection 23
   New board – New beginnings 24
   Learning community: Starting point for
   dialogue 25
   What is meaningful learning? 26
   Relevant resources for change 26
   Checking the pulse 27
   Differences revealed 27
   Figure 1. Antelope Range Belief Statements 28
   Exposing the tensions 28
   Compromise: A risky but fruitful process 29
   A language is born 29
   Responding to resistance 29
   Developing responsive leadership 30
   Behind closed doors 31
   Assistance from the academy 31
   Success – in real life? 32
   Summary 32
   Workshop Questions 34

Chapter Three:
Meaningful Learning Using Technology .37
Interpreting the factors 37
Developing the technology plan 37
Budgeting for implementation 38
Developing strategies for technology
implementation 39
Developing the stop-checks 39
Intentions versus tensions 40
Keys to successful technology implementation 41
Workshop Questions 42

Chapter Four:
Focusing on New Professionalism 45
"Ground Zero" 45
Responding to community expectations
and partnering 46
Developing systemic policy to support
growth, supervision and evaluation 46
Supporting the professional practice 47
Teaching practice made accountable?
An outrage! 47
Developing the common language – again . . .48
Directing the resources and energies 49
Assessing the progress 49
Raising the ante 49
Summary 50
Workshop Questions 51

Chapter Five:
Leadership, Planning and Reporting 53
The planning process: Goals, objectives and
priorities 53
Setting targets – analysis and reflection 54
Table 1: Antelope Range Planning Cycle 55
Linking accountability and growth 55
*Table 2: Antelope Range Sample Student
Achievement Report* 56
*Figure 2. Report on Improvement Goal
Number 1* 56
Principal evaluation – a paradox 57

Workshop Questions 58

Chapter Six:
Small Schools – Bane or Boom? 61
Small school syndromes and symptoms 62
Celebrating the culture 64
Workshop Questions 65

Chapter Seven:
Reflecting and Learning 67
Lessons learned 67
Workshop Questions 71

References 73

Related Readings 77

**Appendix A: Developing the Antelope
Range Beliefs Statement** 79

**Appendix B: Antelope Range Leadership
Capacity Staff Survey (adapted)** 81

**Appendix C: Rubrics for Teacher
Evaluation** 83
*Figure C1. Rubrics for the evaluation of
teachers with Interim Certification
(beginning teachers)* .84

Appendix D: Project Application 91

Appendix E: Frequently Asked Questions . .93

Index 97

Reader's Notes (blank) 98

Acknowledgements

We are indebted to our colleagues with whom we have worked in many schools, school jurisdictions, the Department of Education and, most recently, at the university. In our time, the changes we have witnessed in governance, curriculum, pedagogy, leadership and assessment practices have challenged all of us, and we have been fortunate to have been part of an evolving and continuously improving school system. We are particularly grateful to Dr. George Bedard for his review of our work, and whose suggestions have helped us make the links to the educational leadership context, theory and framework.

Introduction

The nature of school leadership has changed dramatically in recent years. Several initiatives have developed over the past decade calling for a focused, committed, systemic approach to school leadership. Restructuring programs have run rampant throughout North America, and many of these projects have incorporated site-based decision-making, school improvement initiatives, technology support for learning, professionalizing the teaching force and a focus on learning through a cognitive lens. Schools and school jurisdictions are facing these challenges with limited resources, with increased pressure for accountability from a results-hungry public, and with an emerging and changing teaching force.

Professionals in school systems have come to realize that one key to success in meeting the challenge lies in developing competent leaders who understand the issues, who can work cooperatively with the many participants in education, and who can articulate a vision in a results-based, accountability-conscious community. This book provides a narrative that traces the experiences of a growing school system meeting its challenges with a practical look at the realities, excitement, frustrations and sometimes heartache involved when the status quo is no longer acceptable as the norm.

Purpose

The purpose of the book is to provide education leaders at the school, district, ministerial and university levels with a realistic view of the challenges and issues involved in creating a responsive and reflective approach to change. The focus throughout will be on the realities of implementing change and the challenge in sustaining change. The staging and sequencing of the text will provide readers with a structure to assess their own situations and to develop strategies based on a thoughtful approach, engaging the reader as an active learner.

Who is this book for?

Readers are ushered through a journey from a status quo, complacent and a somewhat delusionary, loosely coupled world to a purposeful, systemic, tightly coupled learning community. The processes in establishing shared governance, in profiling the important activity of a school system, and in linking planning, resources and results expose the reader to the real work of a school system in transition. The content is relevant for aspiring and practicing school leaders, for teachers who are curious about how decisions are made to support teaching practice and for the many stakeholders who strive for learning community and shared decision-making. We aim to inspire the education community at large by: citing typical experiences of a school jurisdiction; using real-life problems of leaders, teachers, students, parents and trustees; and recounting the trials and tribulations of undertaking an improvement process.

Preface

The journey of Antelope Range School District, not unlike *The Odyssey*, is fraught with perils, surprises, jubilations and despair. It details the high and low points for other school districts and university leadership programs to learn from their mistakes and successes when they are engaged in such a growth process.

Leading for Change is a practical guide to provide education leaders at school, district, ministerial and university levels with a realistic view of the challenges and issues in creating a responsive and reflective approach to change. It is the story of a superintendent who assumed responsibilities for a small school district in the mid 1990s, and how he dealt with the challenges that lay before him. Specifically, this book will focus on the *everyday* issues and the realities of implementation. It will speak to the failures as well as the successes to illustrate the true learning process, highlighting the humor and the heartache, the trials and tribulations that can result on the road to implementing and sustaining meaningful change.

The audience

The Antelope Range story will appeal to a broad audience. Both practicing educators and graduate students of education, and education leaders at all levels will benefit from the insights, concepts and the leadership tools discussed throughout the text. This general interest book will be helpful primarily in the following ways for:

● Practicing principals, superintendents, school board trustees, teachers and school council members who will recognize the situations that

arise as a small school system tries to implement change on its path to restructuring.

● Professors of leadership development courses, masters and doctoral students, and participants in school leadership development programs, who will find the scenario approach both relevant and revealing. Many of the topics will be presented as useful tools for professional development efforts.

On the micro-political level school board trustees, teachers and school council members will find it helpful in understanding systemic processes and their role in supporting and implementing change. Professors will recognize the theory that permeates the change efforts and, at the same time, they will appreciate the contextual factors that sometimes affect and disrupt initiatives.

The knowledge base

The knowledge base for educational leadership practice is often acknowledged as a juggling act between theory and practice. Readers will recognize the struggle to create learning community, the difficulties with collaborative approaches, the challenges of shared governance, the nuances of professionalizing the teaching force and the rewards for perseverance and vision. These key components of leadership become contentious issues while order, representation and history are challenged in the tumultuous realities of systems thinking and shared decision-making.

The information in the text draws on a sample of first-hand experience, supported by current research, and recent changes in relationships in provincial school systems throughout Canada. Special studies and previous work relevant to the project are found in *Reframing Organizations* (Bolman & Deal, 1991), in *Building Leadership Capacity in Schools* (Lambert, 1998), in *Successful School Restructuring: A Report of the Public and Educators by the Center on Organization and Restructuring of Schools* (Newmann & Wehlage, 1995) and by University Council of Educational Administrators (UCEA) with its initiative to describe the educational administration knowledge base around seven domains (1992). Since the UCEA initiative, the Council of Chief State School Officers (CCSSO) has chosen six standards within which to organize the knowledge, dispositions and performances that are relevant for school leaders (2001). This document provides the basis for struggling or beginning school leaders to inform their practice, and for growing school systems to support leadership initiatives.

All of the content reflects the real experience of implementing change in a school district. Representations of real experiences, events, characters and vignettes are used, albeit with fictitious names to protect identities.

This story captures the challenges of a school district engaged in a growth process. The two authors draw on many years of experience in education – much of which has been spent in school and system administration. This experience, combined with their extensive studies in curriculum and administration in Australia, Great Britain, the United States and Canada, provides a rich and credible background for such a topic.

Structure of the chapters

The staging and sequencing of the text provides readers with a structure to assess their own situations and to develop strategies based on a thoughtful approach, engaging readers as active learners. Each chapter begins with a question designed to focus readers on the chapter topic or the big idea associated with that chapter. The question draws attention to the central theme of the chapter and frames the challenge and issues associated with the topic. Each chapter also ends with a series of questions in the form of workshop topics. Topics will frame the questions for discussion and reflection by using the chapter's content to inform the workshop questions. The questions and problems posed are intended to engage readers in a self-assessment and to provide schools or districts with tools for reflective practice. Readers will be challenged to use the book as an interactive tool to inform learning and to promote reflective practice.

A narrative approach is used to examine the current status of the school district juxtaposed with the accepted practice or theory. Typical school district cases are used to support the discussion, although real names and identities are not used. Figures, tables and models are used to illustrate and highlight the discussion.

Chapter descriptions

Chapter One serves as an introduction. It describes the school district setting, the characters and the challenges when Superintendent Greg assumes responsibilities as CEO for the district in 1997. It addresses the nature and characteristics of a school district content with mediocrity and status quo, and it recounts the enormity of the task of not just challenging the status quo, but replacing it with something worthwhile. It provides the groundwork upon which the system moves forward – determining the starting point and interpreting where the system lies on the chaos continuum. The chapter will present an evaluation process to assess the needs within the context of a school district experiencing a leadership crisis. The tensions associated with change, its purposes and the mindful planning to respond to the circumstances are each profiled in the journey.

Chapter Two, "Establishing Community and Learning Organization," poses the question "How do we establish community around common understandings and shared views of learning?" Superintendent Greg undertakes the task to establish some basic beliefs and principles about learning that could potentially serve as a starting point for a school community about to embark on a reconstruction process.

Most school systems in the Western world have struggled with implementing technology to support meaningful learning. Chapter Three cites the funding challenges, the infrastructure needs, the planning issues and the staff resistance involved in making sustainable changes. Chapter 3 extends the discussion about ways in which students learn with the question, "How can we use technology as a supporting tool for learning?" As Antelope Range addresses key components of planning, funding and architecture, it tackles the re-education and support elements of implementation. The staff attitudes become crucial in Superintendent Greg's scheme for integrating technology seamlessly into the classroom environment. Once again a progression is illustrated, beginning with the prevailing community and staff attitudes and tensions, determining the "adopters," "adapters" and "resisters" of technology, and finally implementing a blueprint for the technology plan.

All of the credible literature published to address restructuring in education refers to support for professional development as the linchpin to successful implementation. Chapter Four exposes readers to the stark realities of systematically promoting and encouraging purposeful professional growth. The Antelope Range story paints a picture of humble beginnings. Teacher evaluation is superficial, professional growth is an isolated, personal matter, and staff development is, at best, languishing. The journey toward building professional community is long, arduous and neverending. Simultaneously, it is a journey that offers rich rewards when done properly. The superintendent's focus is on creating common language and standards for teaching and learning, supporting a vision of teaching and learning with targeted funding, and modeling accepted practice in tangible ways. A step-by-step approach is carefully crafted to move the teachers and administrators in the desired direction, introducing a home grown version of best practices in staff development, including: peer coaching, study groups, job-embedded practice and action research. Antelope Range becomes a school district that identifies and values good teaching. The costs are high, the tensions test the relationships and the goals harness the energy. Is there a payoff?

Accountability has been the driving force behind the public interest in the restructuring movement during the past decade. The disenchantment with public education systems has resulted in a relentless pursuit of results, particularly in the form of student achievement. Chapter Five takes us into the heart of this discussion. The superintendent adopts a strategy to attempt to elevate the importance of the planning process, and to adopt measures that link the district activity purposefully to the goals and vision. Once again, the dialogue around target setting and standards creation causes tension and stress. Accountability seems to raise the ire of many educators, and Antelope Range is no exception. However, the superintendent tries courageously to make the link between accountability and growth. The focus in Antelope Range slowly shifts to one of school improvement. But school improvement is never in evidence until we *measure and report!* Not surprisingly, these two components prove to be obstacles to efforts to complete the planning cycle.

Chapter Six goes right to the heart of a small district culture. The advantages of small schools are counterbalanced with attitudes, dispositions and heritage that sometimes mitigate against change, growth and progress. The superintendent comes to understand the norms of the community and how these beliefs and attitudes are serious influencing factors in the restructuring process. The reflection on the contextual issues, and the analysis of the history of the community provide some important links to the Antelope Range school improvement initiative. The introductory question, "To what extent do cultural norms act as barriers to change, and can these norms be changed?" is profound and prophetic.

The odyssey concludes with the summary chapter that comprises answers and examines the often overlooked but important emerging questions, such as "How can we work to eliminate fragmentation and splintering within our district while sustaining meaningful and purposeful change?" and "Are there components to support change that we are not implementing, or are there ways that we can do better?" Chapter Seven provides a closure to the narrative while at the same time it signals that the work of change is never ending. Antelope Range has come a long way, but we are reminded that, just as the antelope keeps roaming the pastures in search of nourishment, school systems need to be vibrant, focused and committed to renewal and change on an ongoing basis.

The Appendices feature some of the tools referred to within the text. Examples include extracts from handbooks, plans, reports and locally developed rubrics.

About the Authors

The two authors draw on rich experiences in education – teaching at many grade levels, serving in a variety of school and system leadership roles, and currently as professors in teacher education. This experience, combined with their extensive education in curriculum and administration, provides a rich and credible background for restructuring and school improvement topics.

Art Aitken (Ed.D, University of Montana) was a school superintendent for a regional district in the province of Alberta, and now is an educational consultant and sessional university instructor. He has taught in elementary and secondary classrooms for 19 years. He has served as a principal at the elementary, junior and senior high levels for 18 years. He has been a school superintendent for 11 years and has based this book on his experiences as school superintendent. Currently, as a visiting professor, he is developing a Leadership Program at the graduate level at The University of Lethbridge. Recent publications include "Lessons to be Learned from the Alberta Experience: Principals' Reactions to Restructuring," in *The Canadian Administrator* (1998); "In Pursuit of the Next Generation of Basic Education Accountability in Alberta," *International Electronic Journal for Leadership in Learning* (2001); and "AISI and the Superintendent: Opportunities for New Relationships," in proceedings of the *Canadian Society for Studies in Education Symposium* (2000), Edmonton, Alberta, have addressed school improvement practice, accountability at the system level and the principal's response to change.

Nola Aitken (PhD) teaches at the University of Lethbridge, Faculty of Education – one of the highest rated university faculties in Canada – and is Director for the Centre for Assessment Research in Education (CARE) at the University of Lethbridge. Her Masters degree was in Educational Administration taken at San Diego State University and her PhD taken at the University of Alberta was in Elementary Education. She has more than 20 years of teaching experience in elementary and secondary school, two years as a primary school consultant for a school district, five years as a test development specialist with Alberta's Learning Ministry, and 13 years teaching and researching in higher education. Nola has fostered her interest in leadership by researching and teaching assessment of student learning and actively exploring change in curriculum and teaching implementation, most recently illustrated in her latest book, *Forever Better: Continuous Quality Improvement in Higher Education* (2000).

> *"The purpose of leadership is the improvement of instructional practice and performance."*
>
> *Elmore, 2000b, p. 13*

Chapter One

Introduction: Setting the Stage

How does a school system begin to rebuild? Are there strategies for introducing purpose, direction and standards into a school system in chaos? What are the first steps in creating confidence, governance and support for a growing school jurisdiction?

Stormy seas: The foundations for rebuilding

Greg, a school district consultant, after several months of observation, wasn't at all surprised at the sequence of events that were about to occur. Most catastrophic was that Antelope Range Regional Division was about to come to its knees. He had personally witnessed recent developments that suggested that this was a school board in chaos. Antelope Range was a rural education system that had recently brought together six smaller systems into a regional conglomerate. Teething problems prevailed. The superintendent was under attack by his school board and the public for being indecisive – his policy development program had been stalled at the 11th hour. Greg had been acting as a consultant for the superintendent since the jurisdiction had formed nearly three years ago. His work for the school system had been confined to routine day-to-day administration functions such as implementing special education, and occasional trouble-shooting for the superintendent on personnel matters and policy development. He knew that board-superintendent relations were not good. He had strongly supported the superintendent's efforts to introduce policies and practices to guide decisions and to provide purposeful student pro-

grams. He had respectfully warned the superintendent that the board's *laissez faire* approach to managing schools, coupled with the "one-decision-at-a-time" politically motivated practice for making decisions, and the haphazard distribution of central office support service were having a disastrous affect on the potential of this school system to function in support of learning. The media had embraced the controversial developments with delight, branding the board as "dysfunctional," and calling on the Minister of Education to dissolve the board. A recent scandal involving a dispute between a teacher aide and a teacher had also spilled over to the press, and served to add more fuel to the fire. Greg was certainly expecting trouble. But he didn't anticipate that trouble would fall squarely in his lap!

Taking up the challenge

Greg received the call on his cell phone while setting up a display at a convention where he was peddling computers for a supplier – a part time job that he had been doing while completing his doctoral studies. He was summoned to an urgent meeting with the Board Chairperson regarding the future of Antelope Range. Greg's jaw dropped when he arrived at the meeting and was offered the job on the spot as acting superintendent. His predecessor had "walked" following a recent board meeting where the budget vote, yet again, had been defeated!

Greg took stock of the situation. He knew that this was a school system in disarray. Taking over from a superintendent that had been unable to win the support of the board confronted him with serious challenges and hidden perils. He briefly weighed the odds. On the one hand, he was aware of schools that he knew could respond positively to well-grounded leadership; he was excited about the worthwhile programs that needed implementing; and he was confident about his own viability as a leader. He had had recent experience as a superintendent, and in fact, his previous board had been swallowed up in an amalgamation scheme and was now part of another regionalized school system. He knew the Antelope Range #99 jurisdiction well. On the other hand, he knew that the system was reeling from political in-fighting, a strong distrust in leadership, planning that never got off the drawing board and schools operating in isolation. The problem was further exacerbated by board and central office relationships that were punctuated with a lack of mutual confidence and inadequate communication. And, despite his obvious plight and eroding power base, the exiting superintendent did have some support. Such support emanated from principals who were empowered to build community (at least at a rhetorical level), trustees who were able to make their own decisions away from the board table, some central office staff who enjoyed the friendly working relationships without heavy-handed accountability practices and teachers who were free to make their own classroom decisions. These were all comfortable with a superintendent's manner and style that seemingly freed people up to go in their own direction. He was not intrusive and he left teachers and administrators alone unless parents had complaints. Greg knew that his career would come to an abrupt end if he accepted the job and failed to change this culture and eliminate the crippling problems. He also knew that the road to change was fraught with real and imagined perils, and attempts at restructuring this culture could also result in his own demise. What to do? Taking a vital career chance and throwing caution to the wind, he accepted the job offer.

First order of business: Restoring order

At his first board meeting following his appointment, Greg outlined his immediate plan to the board. He recognized that he would need to show strength and provide direction. Accepting the risks accompanying an open soul-searching discussion, and understanding the potential disenchantment of some of the trustees, Greg threw himself into the fray. This board had been used to building their agendas on whims, extending meetings into the wee hours of the morning, block voting in factions and personally using "trustee power" in their own communities. Greg challenged the board to mend its ways and meet its mandate to provide school system leadership; he indicated how agendas were to be set; he advised the Chair, in an open meeting, how to facilitate an orderly debate; he advised trustees that decisions could only be made at the board table (as opposed to the county-counselor model previously practiced); and he informed the board that he would personally conduct a review of central office services and functions. In turn, he expected the board to adopt guiding policies and to ensure that the system had a workable operating budget.*

He had established his immediate expectations! Greg's short-term strategy was to restore order to the school board's operations and, in so doing, send a message that he was anxious to clear the path for establishing a culture that supports learning.

Moore Johnson (2000) suggests that a school district's history of successes and failures shapes the context within which a superintendent operates. Moore Johnson continues on to state that each district has a structure, a culture and "unique constituency that holds various expectations about what kind of leader the district needs" (p. 75). Greg had read the Antelope

---

*The Canadian system of school board governance is built on a strong focus on children and youth in communities. Manzer (1994) speaks of a history of school boards that are committed to supporting democratic values and community governance. It is this commitment that connects the board, the trustee and the community. This is also the commitment that enables trustees to work through difference; to establish protocols and orderly procedures to guide their meetings; to communicate openly; and to listen, seek input and make informed decisions (Hord, 1994).

Range context as one that required some restoration of confidence, and he planned on enabling that transition incrementally. At the same time, he felt that the textbook formulas for success-setting vision, enabling, empowering and so on, would be a highway paved with peril if he didn't attend to building trust and support (Lieberman, Saxl & Miles, 2000). Failure to acknowledge the situation – the politics, the culture, and the bruises and wounds left over from the immediate past, would be hazardous at the very least.

How well are we informed?

Greg knew that initially he would get some latitude – a short honeymoon period, of sorts. He had laid down the gauntlet at the board table and in so doing created some breathing room. The trustees, clearly not happy with the way they had been functioning as a board, had decided to comply with Greg's request for order and respect, and had charged both the budget and the policy committees to get back on track. He knew that he had been given a window of opportunity. He used this window to gather his thoughts and to develop some strategies. Much of the literature on district-wide leadership acknowledged the need for developing a perspective based on a thorough assessment of the context and the politics of the system (Bolman & Deal, 2000a; Brubaker & Coble, 1997; Elmore, 2000a; McAdams & Zinck, 1998; Murphy & National Society for the Study of Education, 2002).

A leader's strategy

Greg felt that he had taken some important first steps. He had addressed some of the more pressing issues at the board level, and, in so doing, had issued some signals that the governance of this school authority was orderly and responsible. Second, he thought that he needed to move quickly on his central office review – the schools were unhappy with the level of support coming from this office, and the board had little confidence in the management processes in place. Third, he determined that he needed to implement a structure to facilitate site-based decision-making within a clearly understood set of parameters – he acknowledged that a successful organization needed to provide a structure to accommodate appropriate input into governance. Having

settled on these three measures, he decided that the rest would have to wait. There was some pressing leadership work to be tackled on the teaching and learning front, but Greg speculated that he needed to introduce a governance and management infrastructure first so that the system could build or re-organize around some sound principles and policies. Done correctly, this infrastructure could become a symbol of the centrality of student learning.

The central office review was conducted in short order. Greg reviewed job roles, checked reporting structures and conducted interviews to get a read on perceptions of effectiveness. The findings, not surprisingly, revealed some strengths, but also some glaring weaknesses. Greg's recommendations included: improving the financial reporting, implementing a tracking system for school budgeting, revising job descriptions and reporting structures, utilizing a more efficient payroll and accounting package, re-negotiating some contracts and re-aligning the secretarial services. Other key support services such as maintenance and transportation were given a mandate to get their houses in order, develop plans to improve communication systems and report improvements to the superintendent by the end of the school year. Greg felt that the central support systems were not adequately aligned with the classroom as the focal point, and that staff did not have a positive track record in dealing with principals' concerns. Marsh (2000) advocates an approach to leadership that stresses the linkage between management support and educational improvement. Greg challenged his central office staff to model this tenet. In his report to the board he indicated that all of the functions in the school system needed to connect to the student – if they were unable to do this, then they were probably not serving any useful function. At the same time, Greg convinced his board that he had the personnel in place capable of implementing these recommendations. This was important because it provided the staff with a vote of confidence, but simultaneously made expectations for improvement very clear. Principals and teachers had been consulted in the review process, so the recommendations were circulated widely throughout the school system to complete the communication loop. The message was out there that issues were being addressed.

Open communication and accountability

Next Greg turned his attention to communication and governance issues. He appointed a task force to devise a system for communicating board agendas and decisions to the school staff and to the media. He was determined to foster an informed public so that issues, trends and results were open and so that the board embraced its accountability responsibilities. To create an infrastructure modeling shared responsibility, Greg acknowledged that he needed to implement a clearly understood policy to support site-based decision-making (SBDM) and decentralized governance. Until now the jurisdiction had been paying lip service only to the concept of community governance. The board had not shown a lot of enthusiasm about divestiture of power. For far too long it had bathed in its self-importance. But, the Department of Learning had issued a clear mandate to decentralize decision-making and to involve schools and their communities in decisions about how to use resources, to determine the nature of the school program and to develop student management policies and practices. Failure to design a structure to respond to this complex process was clearly at the heart of this system's problems. Nobody knew the rules because there weren't any! SBDM was floating around aimlessly and while the concept made for interesting rhetoric, decisions were deferred in some schools, made in others and referred to central office in others. School councils did not have any protocols for operating themselves, and people generally did not understand their roles in the management process.

An action plan

Greg addressed this situation by setting up a series of workshops involving his trustees, principals and community representatives. Despite several attempts at dancing around issues, the territory protection and the victim behavior (remember, this was a school system that was reeling from a lack of confidence and structure), Greg eventually developed a draft SBDM policy from these workshops. The policy clearly identified the various levels for decision-making, the responsibilities accompanying certain decisions and the reporting structure. Imbedded in the policy was a clear delineation of roles and responsibilities and communication processes. The policy provided the structure upon which to make decisions and it left the door open to develop further guidelines to address the specific details and procedures when making shared decisions. He took the draft to his board and he promoted it at the school and community level. He addressed service clubs and parent groups – allowing time for input, reaction and discussion. All the while, he carefully observed responses to this policy and to his other initiatives in the school system. People were becoming engaged in building some frameworks for the organization and thereby developing some ownership at the same time. A good beginning!

Greg felt that some positive progress was unfolding. People in the district were slowly becoming engaged in a dialogue creating ownership for a better future. But, he also was mindful of the magnitude of the task that lay ahead.

Others' agendas, problems, wrinkles and kinks

The early months in the superintendent's position had revealed another curious symptom of a school system in trouble. Greg's phone ran hot! Parents from some of the schools were constantly lining up with complaints – complaints about the principal, about teachers and sometimes about the board and its members. Most were looking for the superintendent to solve a problem involving a student; some were looking to blame someone for a problem; some were seeking a pound of flesh; and some just wanted to tell their story. For a while Greg could not figure out what was causing the flood of calls but he eventually twigged. The reasons were twofold. Some trustees, in their previous role of self appointed overseers, were first of all encouraging parents to bring their school complaints to them (the trustees), and then promptly redirecting them to the superintendent, while sitting in judgment to see how the problem was resolved. Second, some principals were failing to attend to the parents' concerns, thereby exacerbating the frustration so that the parents would turn to the superintendent with the complaint. Greg eventually recognized the game being played. Why leave oneself on the hot seat when one can deflect all the heat to the superintendent? He admonished his principals and informed them that the game was over. Under the new SBDM policy, principals were to take responsibility to help the parent (and student) resolve their own issues. The buck was to stop at the principal's desk. Trustees were advised not to play masters of the universe or to try to act as a clearing-house for school management problems; they were to re-direct the parents back to the principals and to encourage the parents to participate in a school-managed conflict-resolution process. In fact, Greg reminded his trustees that their power was derived at the board table only, and that even though they had important roles away from the board table, making decisions wasn't one of them. It took a whole year to straighten out this problem. By the end of the year the phone calls slowed down, people began to understand the new policy and the superintendent's expectations, and as people accepted their roles, the problems began to get resolved at the level from which they emanated. Finally progress!

Assessing progress and a perception check

Toward the end of the school year, Greg figured that the time was right to assess the progress and check perceptions. He was ready to play his ace. He asked his board to prepare a new contract for him and to address his status as "acting" superintendent, but, at the same time, he insisted that the board open the position to a full-scale competition. While it wasn't exactly what Greg personally wanted, he understood that the board was committed to do this as a condition of his first contract, and second that a clear vote of confidence was essential so that the school system could continue to grow.

It was an interesting experience for Greg, but, more important, the superintendent competition provided the board with a key turning point and an opportunity to demonstrate that internal bickering, factions and feuding were behind them. A few aspirants to the position were experienced superintendents and, no doubt, they brought serious credentials to the table for consideration. Greg was interviewed after each of the other candidates had made their pitch. He used the interview as an opportunity to briefly review what the board had accomplished in the previous few months, how stability had been restored and how some confidence had been developed. But most of all he used the interview as a challenge to the

board to continue on the restructuring path. He insisted that, whereas some groundwork had been laid, the real work was yet to come, and that the board needed to announce their confidence in his initiatives, take pride and ownership for their new way of doing business, and prepare the system for a growth-oriented future. The board bought it, Greg won a new contract, and the board demonstrated solidarity around a common purpose!

First taste of success! Would the next part be so easily accomplished?

Another challenge: Implementing site-based decision-making

Greg was now ready for the next steps. His strategy was to consolidate the SBDM policy by developing and implementing guidelines, to position and align resources to support teaching and learning, and to develop a new three-year plan that would address these and other issues. After a series of meetings and consultations with the community, the new plan was adopted. Greg began with the first important step – hiring personnel that were attuned to the centrality of teaching and learning. Assistant superintendent Will came on board in a strategic move designed to shift the focus of the system away from politics, resource allocation and day-to-day problem solving toward a purposeful holistic plan to enhance the quality of teaching in the district. This move provided a vehicle for a shift in focus. It was a paving stone for a path toward building the district around common purpose, shared vision and mutual cooperation.

So far, what had been accomplished?

The first steps had been taken to *restore order* and to stabilize a school system in chaos. The end of the school year had rolled around and Greg and his board reflected on their progress. The Chief Executive Officer position had been consolidated and the board had expressed confidence in the new leadership; steps had been taken to focus the central office support services on a support role for student learning; board meetings allowed for differences to be debated respectfully and for decisions to be made in a timely fashion; plans were developed to distribute the resources to support instructional goals; and *a functional SBDM policy was positioned to support decentralization* of key decisions. The media were silent (in small communities this is usually an indication that things are going well!). Antelope Range was beginning to function as a school system. But, as one might surmise, the work had only just begun....

Workshop Questions:

1. Decide on the key elements of a site-based decision-making policy for your school system. What are the roles and responsibilities for each site? Describe the sites in your school system (Are transportation, maintenance and administration independent sites with the same management and decision processes as each school site?) What are the planning and reporting structures within your policy? Create a decision-making matrix showing which decisions are site-based, which are central office and which are shared.

2. Develop a set of guidelines for shared decision-making in your school system. Identify three key decision-making areas such as special education, planning and budgeting. Establish guidelines for the processes and roles for making and implementing these shared decisions.

3. Imagine you were to win a contract to evaluate the functions in a school district central office. Describe the parameters, the methodology and the services to be evaluated for such an endeavor. Prepare an instrument that you would use to gather perceptions data on some central office functions.

4. Design a "constitution" for a school council. Include statements that outline representation, conduct of meeting and roles of the council. Include a description of communication processes and how relations are expected to work with the principal, the staff and the board. Show how the work of the council is connected to school improvement.

> *A dragon at the door is the fear that many people have of change. What makes it really complex is that not everyone views change in the same way. For some people in the system...a particular initiative may be seen as an opportunity. For others, it may be seen as a threat – it becomes their dragon at the door.*
>
> Brown & Moffett, 1999, p. 68

Chapter Two

Establishing Structures for Community and Learning Organizations

How can a small school system utilize purposeful leadership to create a teaching and learning culture and a learning community that responds to student needs?

Community – without a purpose?

The stabilizing year had provided ample opportunities for the various participants in the system to express views, to establish routines and to otherwise signal and reflect the values of the system. But, in the course of the many jurisdictional meetings – board, administrator and community – the discussions had not revealed to Superintendent Greg any discerning picture of people's beliefs about learning. In fact, there was little evidence in the conversations that reflected any common beliefs addressing curriculum interpretations and pedagogy relevant to teaching and learning. It was difficult, if not impossible, to glean any understandings about purpose or direction (Barth, 2001). The language tended to be superficial and conservative. What did emerge frequently was that people generally spoke fondly and somewhat defensively about valuing education, about good teaching that revealed a penchant for the basics and about an absence of "big-school" problems. Implicit in this discussion was the assumption that "We are getting it right!"; "Our results are O.K."; and, "We're still doing what we've always done, and it seems to be working." The explicit intention of many of these remarks was that "We are comfortable speaking in platitudes" and, "It's easy to ride the wave of uninformed contentment and self-satisfaction." Greg observed that this was a status quo organization that was stuck in a rut and

lacked commitment and vision. He had employed all of the tools of the trade advocated by Boleman and Deal (2000b) to read the culture: watching, sensing, listening, interpreting and even using intuition – but he had come up with a discomforting pattern that would require his full attention.

Current practice – A paucity of introspection

"The myth is that learning can be guaranteed if instruction is delivered systematically" (Smith, 1986, p. ix).

It occurred to Greg that the dialogue was ill informed, lacked a credible data base from which to draw conclusions and certainly was void of any depth or understanding about curriculum and its nuances. There was no notable celebration of successful learning and neither was there an understanding about achievement in an authentic sense. More particularly there was no apparent sense of community that informed teaching and defined learning – a serious failure to capitalize on the potential that a rural education system offered. Greg was convinced that Antelope Range had no systematically articulated understanding about what constituted good teaching, and neither was there a common belief about effective learning in particular. The original Antelope Range notion of site-based leadership had actually produced a system characterized by obscure purpose, innocuous goals and misdirected accountability. The mission statement, "Education for all in Learning Communities," had a ring to it that supported a site-based approach, but the school system behavior demonstrated no discernable understanding of "learning community," let alone a systematic approach to enact that statement and all that it stood for. The leaders in the district were actually running a masquerade and had used site-based decision-making as a tool behind which to hide. Nobody could articulate what the school jurisdiction stood for, what was important or how to recognize what or when it was "doing well." Worse, key leaders in the system resisted, either actively or passively, any attempts to dialogue about effective learning. Some manifested this resistance by choosing to remain stubbornly silent when prompted to articulate goals. A few opposed any suggestion to create a common focus because it violated the sanctity of site-based decision-making; and yet others paid lip service to narrow definitions of effective learning – without any real understanding about the pedagogy to which they referred.

In short, the school district lacked common purpose and the strength of leadership necessary to capitalize on an empowered system of governance and learning community. This was a loosely coupled, loosely regulated and loosely connected school system. Greg knew that one of those "looselys" had to change! The strategy for change had to be simple and localized. Greg sensed that many change efforts died on the table when leaders try to import a winning formula and apply it in a "cookie-cutter" manner regardless of local circumstance (Wheatley, 2000).

New board – New beginnings

The situation came to a head immediately following the election of a new board of trustees in the fall of 1998. Following the year of stabilizing and confidence building [outlined in Chapter 1], Greg knew that this was the opportune time for some decisions regarding moving the jurisdiction ahead and identifying a common purpose. With a newly elected board in place, Greg sensed that progress could be made with the sanction of a board anxious to stake its claim to "cleaning up" the system. More importantly, Greg also knew that trustee support was essential if there were to be a move toward accountability and commitment.

In collaboration with the board, Greg arranged for the trustees to tour each school in the district. The thought was to "drop-in" at each school, meet the staff in an informal setting on their own turf, shake hands with any parents who happened to be in the school and visit a few classrooms to see how the students were taking care of business. What transpired during that "tour" provided Greg with convincing evidence that the values in Antelope Range about teaching, learning and community differed considerably from that which had he envisaged about a learning community. He saw learning community, as did Dufour and Eaker (1998), as an opportunity to focus on growth and improvement – based on shared ideas, achievement goals and reflective practice, and with common vision and beliefs (pp. 25-29). During the tour the trustees proved to be a co-operative and congenial lot. Each "local" trustee took turns puffing out his or her chest and profiling "my school," and proudly referring to cleanliness, orderliness and staff dedication. In fact, Greg noted that in most classes during that visit, students were typically passively involved in completing workbook pages – and usually with the whole class working in consort on the same "one-size-fits-all" exercise. The only classroom conversations heard (and those were in a very few instances) were one-sided – where the teacher would be giving a few directions. Certainly no students were caught speaking at all during the tour. There was no teacher-student interaction, absolutely no dialogue between students, no evidence of technology being used as an enhancement, but, instead, there was everything to indicate that the jurisdiction shared a common purpose that valued a stifling, unimaginative and, at best, "traditional" learning culture, that was perhaps perfectly suited to the 1950s. The emphasis was on teacher-delivered, text-focused sources of information, which were best imparted with a "one-right-way" approach, and, at worst, a gross misrepresentation of purposeful curriculum. Although the trustees didn't voice their concerns, Greg was beginning to feel embarrassed by being responsible for a system that lacked meaningful purpose, one that was steeped in mediocrity and was void of accountability to the learner.

Perhaps ironically, the district's achievement data generally supported and reinforced the complacency! Traditional literacy levels were better than average, particularly in the early grades, and pass rates were high, with only moderate problems with science and math at the Grade 12 level. Results on mandated provincial achievement tests (Grades 3, 6 and 9), and on diploma examinations (Grade 12) were classed by the province as satisfactory. Greg was to later find out that, although capable, Antelope Range students generally did not do well on higher order questions. In other words, the students had no trouble managing the lower order (comprehension and recall) questions, but they didn't do well on application, synthesizing information and analysis. This school system had become smug – not moving in any direction, let alone ahead – and people were taking pride in creating a suffocating, staid learning environment, characterized by a limited "coverage" philosophy (Gardner, 1991) and a mindless drift into complacency. Nobody seemed to care or acknowledge that the outside world had changed. It was the turn of the millennium and students were not being adequately challenged and prepared for this information age, and the system was failing to capitalize on its resources.

Sadly, tapping into student potential and teaching for depth of understanding was not a priority in Antelope Range.

Learning community: Starting point for dialogue

Greg decided that it was time to take action and he determined that he needed to start with the governing body of the school system. He took the matter up with his board. He tried to articulate an interpretation to his trustees that exposed this school system for what it was. He also cited freely from a public consultation study completed by the provincial School Board Association in 2001: "...a significant number of respondents felt that the school should insist on a higher standard than was evident and displayed in the community" (p. 7). This was a study that involved a population sample from ratepayers of public school boards across the province. As one respondent noted, "community values and standards are too low" (p. 7). The study also commented on the need for home, school and community to support and assist each

other in shaping young people into good citizens. In an editorial comment the School Board Association president remarked that the school would not be successful if the home and community do not support the values and standards it wishes to communicate to, and instill in, the students. Conversely, the home and community would not be successful if the school did not support them.

When confronted with issues of lack of relevance, students ill-prepared for a different workplace and the prospect of graduates devoid of appropriate communication skills, the board agreed that this was not the type of education that it wanted to provide for Antelope Range students and neither was it the type of education suggested in the public consultation. Greg had worked with this school system in the superintendent capacity by now for more than one year. The returning trustees had watched the manner in which Greg had gone about his work. They were able to share with their new trustees that Greg was a leader who, above all, was an advocate of effective teaching and purposeful learning. The board chairperson insisted that Greg was a leader to be trusted – his practices and initiatives would be based on improving the system. In turn, Greg committed to including the board in making the key decisions regarding the future of this system. There was clearly an implicit trust between this superintendent and his board. There was a tentative acknowledgement that students could effectively learn the content by being encouraged to *think* about what they knew, to *formulate essential questions*, and *to inquire about possible answers* by appropriate use of resources. Trustees agreed that *deep* understanding was preferable over superficial "made-to-order" learning (Knight, Aitken & Rogerson, 2000). With this in mind, the trustees gave the superintendent a green light to take the necessary steps to inject some life into the school system and to create a learning community based upon common beliefs, shared goals, high standards of teaching and a focus on student achievement. The board expressed confidence in this initiative based on Greg's explanation about how there is a worldwide focus on making a difference for students, and the difference being about school improvement, strengthening and deepening leadership, building professional learning communities and improving opportunities for children (Carter, 2002). Greg knew that this was to be a formidable task that would take time, astute strategy and commitment. But the board's acknowledgment of the direction was an important first step in creating a system in transition and moving towards a culture that values learning.

Greg's view about creating a learning organization was that it needed to emerge from a messy, complex environment. He consulted Fullan (1997) and understood that he would need to pick and choose his way in attempting to use certain events as "catalysts for action," and turn obstacles into opportunities. The board, albeit in crude fashion, had essentially created the vision. Greg's job as superintendent was to model his commitment to student learning, and to use well-chosen strategies to implement the vision.

What is meaningful learning?

The central office leadership team spent some time examining the factors that made up the profile of this school jurisdiction including (1) leadership, (2) standards of teaching and (3) criteria for achievement – searching for the components that triggered the complacency. The team concluded that the system was wanting in each of these important areas. Greg decided that the starting point had to go right to the heart of the meaning of education. A check on the documentation supporting restructuring in the provincial system revealed that jurisdictions, and indeed schools, were encouraged to "decide upon their own methodology and philosophy about teaching and learning in consultation with the community – so long as it produced results" (Alberta Education, 1995). There is a certain amount of merit in this approach in that, when done properly, according to Perkins (1992), it does promote local ownership and it does recognize internal contextual variables that inform the teaching and learning process (p. 16). However, if it is not applied in a responsible manner, it can become what it had indeed become in Antelope Range – a system of education that revered orderliness, that discouraged staff from considering credible research findings and that fostered a parent community that was not really involved in any meaningful way. Student feedback on district satisfaction survey results gave a strong indication that teaching was uninspiring, teacher-centered and boring.

Greg's conclusion and starting premise was that the system stakeholders all needed to get in touch with fundamental beliefs and understandings about effective teaching and learning, and with how professional learning communities actually function. Consequently, this question was posed throughout the system: What are the important understandings about effective teaching and learning in Antelope Range?

The central office team (Greg and Will) chose a fan-out discussion process to determine the Antelope Range position on this matter, depending on the principals to facilitate a dialogue within their schools and communities. The principals' group was to lead the discussion, solicit the views of staff and community, and eventually generate a system-wide statement. At the same time that this work was launched, a similar process was being implemented to focus on teacher evaluation standards and to review related policies and practices (Chapter Four), to develop a technology plan (Chapter Three) and to implement a new system-wide planning cycle (Chapter Five). In each of these instances, principals were expected to promote and encourage dialogue. For example, Greg asked the principals to facilitate the teaching and learning discussion in their school communities and to engage staff and parents in a dialogue about what they valued in learning. He also asked them to participate in the research process, debate their perceptions with colleagues at the principals' table and to work toward consensus. They didn't appear to be daunted by the enormity of the task but, on the other hand, their silence and unwillingness to clarify the directions should have tipped off Greg that their confidence and ability to respond to this challenge might be lacking.

Relevant resources for change

Intervention was critical at this point. Greg brought some of the relevant learning community literature to the table for review and discussion. Research on school improvement (DuFour & Eaker, 1998) on building school culture (Bolman & Deal, 1997) and on systemic change (Fullan, 1999) helped focus the discussion on the jurisdiction's mission statement: "Education for All in Learning Communities." After some deliberation principals all conceded that they were indeed part of a learning community – but a community made up of several smaller learning communities. Carefully navigating through this discussion, Greg led the principals to agree that they needed a unifying element and model from the learning community at large – the Antelope Range learning community – and this common purpose should give impetus to the overall system. By working toward the community-at-large concept, Greg was seeking to hold schools accountable to a broader, common purpose. Principals began to see that if they agreed on a common purpose, perhaps the system could employ resources and energies in an effective way to support the common purposes – and in turn strengthen and bring focus to the "local" learning communities. This discussion reinforced and clarified the jurisdiction mission and provided a launching pad for the groundwork that was to follow. Following this mission statement review, Greg turned the attention of the group to determine what was important about the key function of the school system – *teaching and learning*.

Checking the pulse

What transpired was an ongoing and sometimes spirited debate about components of effective teaching and learning. Most of the concern and tension centered on the role of the teacher and the responsibilities of the students and parents. Greg tried to keep recent research and new understandings to the fore (ASCD Yearbook, 1997), and to focus the discussion on beliefs about learning. He challenged participants to focus on the learner audience, how students best learn, roles and responsibilities, assessment practices, relationships and communication. This had the effect of reducing the distracters and minimizing the efforts of some to introduce extraneous factors to the discussion – red herrings such as governance, leadership and politics – although Greg certainly acknowledged that each of those factors also impacted on learning. Some of the research cited in the discussion emanated from Hargreaves (1998) regarding changing conditions that affect teaching, Slee (2000) to inform the inclusive education dialogue, and Caine and Caine (1994) and Perkins (1992) to introduce cognitive development and brain-based learning into the equation. Greg was determined to focus the debate on matters that directly addressed sound teaching and learning principles.

Differences revealed

Following this discourse the principals chose nine draft statements that they perceived to represent the important components of effective learning. The draft statements were circulated to schools and school councils for discussion and input (Appendix A). Greg knew that many of the statements were superficial, but this represented the work of his school community, so he was determined to privilege the effort. The response was, not surprisingly, quite mixed. Most staffs were either satisfied with the statements or simply chose not to respond. Similarly most school councils accepted the principals' view of learning. However, a few school councils – those that tended toward the right-wing conservative end of the spectrum – challenged the notion of developing responsible and thoughtful learners. They argued that a student-learner's role was to passively accept the doctrine of the teacher, and at the same time, to also take full responsibility for learning the content (most typically by memorizing facts). This discussion proved to be the linchpin that unlocked the "differences" prevailing within the Antelope Range communities.

The teacher's role, professionalism and student achievement became the focal points of the dialogue. Greg welcomed the debate because it was his first indication that some people in the system were prepared to articulate a belief and defend it, albeit quite often without substantial support from research. But the difference in opinion did provide a focal point for the discussion. It did expose some disagreement about fundamental purposes of school; it certainly uncovered differences in interpretation of curriculum; and it did ultimately require considerable compromise to come to agreement. The end result was a set of statements that reflected the Antelope Range position or beliefs about learning. The specificity regarding pedagogy and epistemology weren't there, but Greg thought that the statements could provide a foundation for further development and dialogue within the learning community. He also believed that the collaborative process had exposed some key issues and it was time to test the statements at the staff and community levels. The results of the beliefs statement work follow.

Figure 1. Antelope Range Belief Statements

Antelope Range Regional Division prepares students to develop into life-long independent learners and productive community members who take responsibility for their own actions and are considerate of others. The following beliefs about learning are the foundation that supports all we do toward that end.

In a learning community:

1. Every person is capable of learning.

2. Every person respects the dignity of others.

3. Home and community play a vital role in the learning process.

4. The learner-teacher relationship is the core to the school experience.

5. Learning is an engaging activity and is negotiated in a safe and secure environment.

6. Education, which encompasses the process of learning, is a shared responsibility.

7. Every person in our system is valued and learns in a unique way.

8. Accountability to student learning is the core business at all levels of school system operations.

9. Success in learning is accomplished by balancing academic achievement with an appropriate emphasis on the emotional, physical, creative and social development of the student.

Exposing the tensions

Visions which tap into an organization's deeper sense of purpose, and articulate specific goals that represent making that purpose real, have unique power to engender aspiration and commitment. To be genuinely shared, such visions must emerge from many people reflecting the organization's purpose (Senge, 1994, p. 299).

During the process of examining and articulating each belief it became evident that the interpretative practice of compromise was fraught with difficulties. There were those who had an agenda to protect a traditional type of teaching that placed the teacher at the centre of the learning process: "The teacher's knowledge was the curriculum"; and "The teacher's word was final and indisputable," they said. Underlying this principle also was the notion that the teacher deserved respect – no matter what! The counter argument represented an ethical liberal perspective (Manzer, 1994) advocating a learner-centered approach – building on the student's understanding, engaging the student in teacher-facilitated construction of knowledge and having the teacher take responsibility for determining, and responding to, the uniqueness of the learner.

The productive aspect of the debate was that it became readily apparent who stood on each side of the issue and who was uncommitted. But, for some, developing belief statements was viewed as a political activity or a power play more than as a pedagogical endeavor. An example of a source of discomfort for some was the implication of recognizing that every student was capable of learning – a notion that directly challenged teacher accountability and one that implicitly required a focus on learner needs. These tensions punctuated the compromise process, but persistence guided the discussion from draft statements to a final document for board consideration.

Greg was reminded that the real work in vision implementation was in the space between the goals and the current status. Senge (1994) states that the gap between vision and current reality is a source of energy. "Creative tension [is] the innate pull that emerges when we hold clear pictures of our vision juxtaposed with current reality" (p. 299).

Things had certainly heated up in Antelope Range. The "lope" in Antelope Range had at least become a canter!

Compromise: A risky but fruitful process

The central office leadership team had orchestrated a compromise process that had provided a basis for developing learning community. The statements might not have quite transcended the gap between Antelope Range practice and an ideal world, but they were a potential beginning to establishing learning community built around shared purpose. The team felt it important that the final statements were worded in such a way that most schools and most teachers in the system could respond competently within the framework of the beliefs and yet still choose teaching methods based on differing needs of students. Principals could use these statements appropriately as tools to focus on improving learning and other school improvement initiatives. The beliefs lent themselves ideally as a discussion prompt for school councils and parents. Teachers could use the beliefs as an interpretive tool to determine pedagogy and to reflect on how their comfort zones linked to the statements' intentions. District leaders could refer to the beliefs as agreed-upon statements to drive planning, growth and enhanced student achievement. The statements could provide the foundations for a new Antelope Range culture that focused on purposeful teaching and learning. Greg felt that the system had taken its first step in the restructuring journey.

A language is born

"Human life is rationalistic in that it operates on the assumption that human life might be made intelligible, accessible to human *logos* or reason, in a broad or full embodied sense" (van Manen, 1990, p. 16). In other words, language and thinking, both derived from the same root, *logos*, are therefore difficult to separate (Gadamer, 1990; Heidegger, 1977; van Manen, 1990). It is important to understand that language is not only dealing with words as in the nominal sense, but with the meaning *behind* the words. It is crucial then, that in attempting to secure a common understanding among people with diverse lived experiences, that language does not get in the way of that understanding but instead, acts as a vehicle *for* understanding. This notion became clear to the trustees when they realized that these beliefs, viewed as

agreed-upon statements, provided a common language to inform the planning and results discussions.

The school board reviewed the work and, after careful consideration, cautiously endorsed the product. The trustees commented that they now had a language that they could use when talking to teachers. The beliefs could become a focal point for board planning and problem-solving. On the other hand the reality of implementation also set in! It quickly became apparent that the belief statements were not accepted by many of the teaching staff. It seemed that the fan-out discussion process had not effectively captured their interest and support – and, more importantly, neither had it provided an outlet for disagreement. District data such as student achievement, teacher evaluation reports, teacher growth plans, satisfaction surveys and principal supervision reports continued to strongly suggest to the superintendent and the board that change was slow and that the belief statements were considered to be a "board" document or perhaps, at best, an administrator lever to be resisted. Frustrating as this was, Greg realized that much more effort and purposeful strategy was needed to make headway with the mission and to meet the goals of the system. To reinforce the doctrine of the beliefs, the central office team consistently brought conversations, meeting discussions and teacher dialogue back to the language of the beliefs statements. In this way the team tried to model the value of encouraging practice that was purposely informed by the system-wide understandings. But these efforts were having only marginal impact at the classroom level. Something more was needed. But, what?

Responding to resistance

The collaborative process to develop the beliefs had exposed some problems in the system. There had been some fundamental flaws uncovered in the way that the consultation process had been implemented throughout the jurisdiction. A few principals had diligently sought input and had promoted discussion. Others had engaged neither their school staff nor the parents, and certainly not their students, in the beliefs discussion. In some cases the work was simply passed on as "information," thereby failing to promote the desirable dialogue. The attitude from this corner was captured in the remark (albeit off the record) made by one principal, "This too shall pass!" Yet others neglected to present and represent the draft statements to the staff. Some even used the work as a tool (or weapon) to establish a line of defense. The line of thinking in this group went something like this: "How can we work around this?" "How can we undermine this such that it won't disrupt our comfort zone?" Upon reflection the central office administrative team members recognized these practices and tactics, and they doggedly put their heads together to think of ways to enact the beliefs and to use them effectively to link the ongoing work of the school system. Leithwood, Jantzi and Steinbach (1999) found that successful initiatives had a lot to do with the openness of the leaders and their modeling of cooperative and collaborative practices. Recognizing the flaws in the collaborative process, they decided to focus on the factor that had undermined the effectiveness of the process – indeed the factor that had reduced the site-based policy to a travesty – *leadership*. If Antelope Range were to create a meaningful learning community, then strong leadership would be necessary to bring focus and purpose to the system.

Developing responsive leadership

Again Greg consulted with the board. Trustees were disappointed that leaders in the system had not been committed during the collaborative process and they recognized that Antelope Range could not respond to 21st Century challenges without appropriate leadership. The board also recognized that the success of its empowerment initiative through its site-based policy depended on reliable leadership.* How then could the system help develop the accountability that seemingly was missing? The board was anxious to see improved student achievement results and felt that leaders in the schools were accountable for bringing about the changes that would produce these results. Greg helped his board understand that there needed to be a fundamental shift in leadership practice if it were to adequately prepare students for an information age. As Murphy (1992) states: "[L]eaders and leadership in the postindustrial age must look radically different from what they have looked like in the past" (p. 124). He also invoked the work of Kouzes and Posner (2002):

---

*A contemporary view in education holds that leadership is informed and shaped by a transformational model that has its origins in management literature but has been applied, studied and embellished in educational settings. Such a model sees the building of vision, strategy, capacity and commitment in the service of the learning community as the key role of formal leadership, with various formal and informal leadership roles shared by teachers in a distributive framework (Leithwood et al., 1999; Murphy, 1994). Acknowledged components of the transformational model include:

Establishing vision

Setting goals

Communicating high expectations

Supporting initiatives

Stimulating intellectual growth

Modeling commitment

Creating a learning-oriented, inquiry-based culture

Structuring the organization

The new view of leadership is supported by the emerging understandings about school culture (Barth, 2000; Deal & Peterson, 1999), and about professional learning community (Hord, 1997b). These frameworks draw particularly on a complex and dynamic school environment characterized by change, growth and continuous improvement. The organizational aspects are supported by an underlying drive to build a capacity where relationships and commitment are focused on accountability to student achievement (Jackson, 2000; Lambert, 1998; Spillane & Seashore Louis, 2001). Fundamental to this complex arrangement is a focus on teacher development to enhance the skills to work collaboratively and to learn and grow (Blase & Blase, 1998; Sparks & Hirsh, 1994). Marsh (2000) claims "leaders in restructured schools work in educational systems which are increasingly tightly coupled around results and loosely coupled around means for attaining these results" (p. 131).

Rather than view leadership as an innate set of character traits – a self-fulfilling prophecy that dooms society to having only a few good leaders – it's far healthier and more productive to assume that it's possible for everyone to learn to lead. By assuming that leadership is learnable we can discover how many good leaders there really are. (p. 387)

The board warmed up to the task. Greg received full board support to plan a leadership development program that would meet the needs of the system and promote individual development and professional community amongst its leaders. Again at the principals' meetings, selected leadership literature was revisited. Principals agreed that a learning community can only flourish with strong leadership, but all were quick to acknowledge that shared leadership was desirable where schools were small, tasks were diverse and resources were limited. Greg introduced Lambert's (1995) work to the group, providing all the principals with a copy of *Building Leadership Capacity* to read – so the leadership development work could begin in earnest. Greg and his central office colleagues were determined to raise the level of principal commitment to the collaborative process.

Behind closed doors

An interesting development occurred just about at this time. The principals started conducting private or closed meetings before the regular monthly system-wide principal meetings. It was clear that the intent of the closed meetings was to anticipate some of the agenda discussion with a view to organizing support or opposition to particular "central office" initiatives, or to focus on common concerns and thereby use the principal meeting agendas as a forum for complaints. For a while, it made for interesting discussion. Greg was pleased that some principals who had previously been silent started to participate in the meetings, although usually with somewhat shallow and sometimes capricious vagaries: "I agree with that side of the table!" or, "I can live with that!" or, "My staff feels the same way!" Others became quite vociferous as they "led the charge," championing their pet peeve – or the peeve that had been assigned to them by the "meeting before the meeting."

The central office team consistently facilitated the discussion by turning comments back to the principals for clarification and critique as people were challenged to substantiate their perspectives and observations, and were frequently asked to frame their concerns within the context of the belief statements about teaching and learning. The principals were growing and developing as a group – not always together, but at least now they were able to disagree, to voice their concerns and to take a stance on issues. Greg considered that challenging principals to confront their assumptions was ultimately essential to developing leadership capacity in Antelope Range.

Assistance from the academy

Greg decided that the time was right to build on this new willingness to dialogue. Again, after careful consultation within the central office team and the board, he contracted a university professor to facilitate some leadership development with the principals. The board strongly believed that leadership was the key factor for success in such a far-flung community as Antelope Range. The consensus was that the site-based decision-making policy, coupled with a new teacher evaluation process that was built on supervision of teaching practice and personal teacher growth rather than an evaluation cycle, meant that the principal's role needed to be a much enhanced one. Indeed, the board was of the opinion that the Antelope Range investment in student learning and results could only be as strong as its leaders' convictions. As a result the board contracted Professor Rhodes from one of the province's universities to facilitate a leadership development program.

Professor Rhodes was encouraged to use Lambert's work in *Building Leadership Capacity* (1995) to provide the principals with a tool for self-reflection. The leadership development team – Greg, Rhodes and Assistant Superintendent Will – designed a questionnaire, using Lambert's model, to help principals measure the leadership capacity in their own local learning communities (Appendix B). As a preliminary to the survey, Greg informed the principals that shared decision-making, collaboration and visioning were important, but only contributing parts of an overall capacity-building process, and that these elements of the process needed to be purposefully linked by facilitative leadership.

Success – in real life?

Despite the heroic efforts of Professor Rhodes, the discussion went flat. Only one principal accepted the challenge to invite Rhodes into his school to work with school staff on building an empowerment culture and professional community. Although a few responded to the questionnaire, the data were never brought back to the table for consideration. Greg had not pushed hard enough on this issue. The principals had only partially used the survey – many had not taken the request seriously and therefore had not distributed the survey to staff. The principals met Rhodes' challenges with stunned silence, not unlike antelope that had been caught in the headlights. However, despite this setback, Greg was not totally disappointed with the leadership development efforts. Several gains were being made. For example, the technology coordinator and Assistant Superintendent Will had developed a technology plan that had required extensive consultation and collaboration throughout the system. The principals had supported this important venture (Chapter Three). Second, an annual planning process had been adopted and implemented. Principals played a key role in this endeavor (Chapter Five). Third, the standards for teaching had been developed, and rubrics for assessing competency levels were being developed in a collaborative process with principals (Chapter Four). Each of these developments was supported by considerable discussion and dialogue both at the principals' table and throughout the system, and leadership development was happening more as a matter of course than as a result of a distinct and separate endeavor. Greg was encouraged and felt that the learning within the context was starting to pay dividends.

Even though the response to the visiting professor's efforts to enhance leadership capacity had been lukewarm at best, the leadership work in Antelope Range was moving ahead. Clearly some important gains had been made. Throughout the beliefs statement development process, and as a result of the continuous need for collaboration and commitment in the subsequent dialogue that accompanied each of these new initiatives, the Antelope Range principals had learned that this school system was developing its own form of learning community. All of the collaborative work had a strong student focus. People realized that the beliefs statements were having a springboard effect because some of the statements were used to launch other initiatives, to inform planning and to dialogue about learning issues in schools. This was a beginning to developing common purpose in shaping the Antelope Range infrastructure around purposeful tenets. The leadership workshops and the focus of principals' meeting agendas had become quite student focused. Different viewpoints were embraced as an opportunity to confront assumptions and to reflect on professional practice. The language of learning community was beginning to permeate the discussion at the board table, the principals' forums, the faculty lounges and some parent council agendas.

Antelope Range, in the span of about 18 months, had moved from its status quo approach to a world in transition. It was a world that could respond to students' needs, could plan for a better future and could build itself around informed dialogue and reflective practice. It was a world that was based on agreed-upon principles about learning.

Summary

Now the beliefs about teaching and learning in Antelope Range tended to be a mixture of shallow, flavor-of-the-day, and anachronistic statements that lacked the conviction of authentic collaboration, but regardless, they were beliefs. The development of the statements was based on an either-or understanding (limited as it was) of practice and theory. This bifurcation of theory and practice created insular professionalism that was unaccountable to current learning theory. The beliefs were loosely coupled and loosely regulated, but this approach was an accepted norm in a school system that had accepted a developing interpretation of learning community.

The leadership development enterprise in Antelope Range was viewed as the foundation for all of the system improvement initiatives. The initial step involved developing an understanding of how a district might begin to build a capacity for growth and improvement and to create a learning culture responding to learner needs in the information age. The collaboration and dialogue revealed that narrow interpretations of accountability and selected forms of empowerment had a deleterious effect on the results of leadership. However, the discussion did have the effect of exposing some misunderstandings, revealing some of the philosophical stances with respect to learning community, and creating a base for more developmental work.

The work in establishing common purpose and shared meaning is long and arduous – and it is ongoing. The whole idea of nurturing professional learning communities is contingent upon a sustained and committed effort (Aitken, Gunderson & Witchen, 2000). Recipe approaches to change might prove to be useful in kick-starting an initiative – but have limited sustainable value. It became clear that Antelope Range needed purposeful strategies to encourage, support and fully implement change. The move toward a learning community required a partnership commitment that needed to be fostered and nurtured throughout all of the work in the school system.

Workshop Questions:

1. How can a school respond to individual student needs in an empowered setting, and yet still buy in to the ideals of the learning community at large?

There are at least three questions to be considered here. Perhaps three different task committees could be struck to research each component and report back to the group at large.

Committee 1: How can the principles of empowerment be employed to the students' advantage in a school setting?

Committee 2: To what extent do individual student needs impact on our teaching practice?

Committee 3: How can professional learning community principles enhance student learning?

Following the committee work, articulate a draft plan for implementation that cites school approaches supporting the larger learning community. Identify strategies for involving partners and coordinating the school plan with the school system at large.

2. How can a principal support a learning community that calls for shared vision, goals-based thinking and systemic strategies, if the principal fundamentally disagrees with the system beliefs about teaching and learning?

(Hint: Think of a very short and uncomplicated answer!)

3. As a staff, write your own belief statements about teaching and learning. Consider the curriculum planning, pedagogy, epistemology, classroom management, student achievement, community roles and responsibilities, and leadership, together with the role that each has with effective learning practice. How will you facilitate the process and involve the stakeholders in your school?

This is one that really can't be tackled with a committee approach. The whole-group discussion needs a skilled facilitator to tease out the understandings and the interpretations. Research teams could then be assigned to learn about current developments and provincial policies, and task teams could be assigned to break down and analyze the school's data (Slavin, 2003). The process needs to be staged with care so that there are extensive opportunities for discussion and reflection and consultation.

4. Design a school improvement plan that focuses on raising school achievement in mathematics (for example). How will you determine targets, teaching strategies, roles, measures, resources and research to reach your improvement goal?

Think of this one from a professional development perspective. Committees could certainly work well here, and would indeed enhance the professional dialogue as staff members develop expertise in their respective focus areas. The improvement plan will take time to develop and will require extensive collaboration along the way. Research, planning, consultation, monitoring and evaluation are essential parts of the process.

> *"Technology won't replace a teacher but a teacher with technology will."*
> Source Unknown

Chapter Three

Meaningful Learning Using Technology

How can we use technology as a supporting tool for meaningful learning?

Interpreting the factors

Greg and Will were aware of the perils of imposing a technological structure on teachers and schools that required a hands-on approach to using technology. Resistance was bound to run rampant! They were also aware that, left to their own devices, schools would adopt technology in a haphazard fashion, resulting in runaway costs and perhaps having only incidental links to student learning. The Department of Learning was sending a clear mandate to school systems to develop a systematic approach to acquiring and using technology. The painstaking work to develop teaching standards (Chapter Two) had uncovered the need to promote teacher skills and competencies to support learning – particularly with respect to emerging technologies. Antelope Range was caught in a Catch-22 scenario.

Previous attempts to create foundations for a technology plan in the district had been stalled by uncertainty about costs, disagreement about hardware and conflicting research about network systems and protocols. Two locally-appointed task forces had failed to produce a workable plan, and had revealed that Antelope Range lacked the competence and the resources to make informed recommendations. Will researched the state of affairs in other school systems and found a variety of implementation issues of a similar nature. Dialogue with school principals drew mixed responses, but the call for more hardware was

clear. Again, what was not clear was the intended use of such equipment. Greg and Will conducted a full-scale inventory throughout the system to get a handle on the hardware, software, expertise and understanding of the use of technology in their schools. When they analyzed the results their concerns were confirmed. What did they find? Staff were taking stock of their computer inventory and using this superficial activity as an indication of their progress toward adoption of technology in their programs. In fact, schools had no plans for controlling inventory or for teaching computer skills. Worse, skills and competencies were lacking – severely. Adopting technology in a purposeful way would take a serious leadership effort, a carefully researched plan and a bold approach. It was time for action.

Developing the technology plan

This was a crucial time in the development and restructuring of Antelope Range. Greg and Will decided that they needed a two-pronged plan of attack. A technology plan needed to be all encompassing – it had to address learning, teaching, budgets, resource acquisition and maintenance. It needed to reflect a concerted approach to implementing the Information and Communication Technology (ICT) curriculum, which demanded not only preparing teachers with the skills, but also preparing them to adopt pedagogy that would capitalize on the benefits of technology (Sandholtz, Ringstaff & Dwyer, 1997). This work had potential to serve as a vehicle for change, and as a profound influencing factor on effective teaching and community attitudes, if managed adeptly. Greg and Will started to view a technology plan as an opportunity of the first order – an opportunity to focus on relevant teaching and learning experiences, and a creative opportunity to pave the way to an advantage for Antelope Range students. They carefully mapped out a strategy for developing the plan.

As a first step they outlined the proposed direction for the board and won a tentative approval to proceed – but with caution. It was clear that a technology plan would be contentious and reveal some fundamental differences in understanding about effective teaching and learning. Will reminded Greg that it was sure to give voice to skeptics, cynics and critics. At both the board table and at principals' meetings there emerged a view that spending money on technology was a waste, and it hardly supported the need to focus on the basics! This position was consistent with the community conservative element's position in the ongoing discussion about teaching beliefs and standards. On the other hand, there were those who saw technology as an essential tool to enhance learning in a knowledge age – a view supported by the Department of Learning (Alberta Learning, 1999). Knowing that these issues were not going to disappear, the leadership team instructed the technology coordinator to develop a timeline, begin to make some infrastructure decisions and to come up with a plan for consultation with staff and community.

What followed was a process that led Antelope Range down a critical path that committed resources and energies to a new look at teaching practices and student achievement. The initial stages of the plan unfolded without incident. Working from provincial standards, the coordinator recommended a blueprint for stocking the system with modernized computers, and installing a wide area network designed to transmit the signal across the region and to enhance connectivity with the rest of the world. Antelope Range would be in touch with the world via the Internet with high-speed transmission of data into and out of the jurisdiction. Initial discussion about the plan with teaching staff and with the principals' group generally went smoothly, but there were several staff who sat on their hands. That brought Greg to the funding issue.

Budgeting for implementation

There was never any question that a full-scale technology initiative would cost the school system a lot of money. Despite this obvious inference, Greg insisted that the plan be presented to the board with all the details as transparent as possible. He sent Will back to the drawing board to cost out additional facets of the proposal. These included computer replacement programs at every site in the school system – schools, business operations, maintenance and so forth. It included costs of training staff, professional development for teachers and educating the public. To cap it off, Will also included costs of incorporating a distant education model that would permit high school students in small schools to access courses and programs through Internet delivery (this one proved to be the most contentious of all). By the time the "all-included" plan was ready for review, the cost has risen to an average $300 per student per year into the foreseeable future. Considering that the Education Department was funding only a small portion of that amount, this would be a hard sell.

Undaunted, Greg took the plan to the board. There was an immediate heightened awareness and excitement. "This will be a plan that will give Antelope Range students learning opportunities beyond our wildest dreams," said the elated Board Chairperson. Trustees were equally excited! But then they paused to consider the impact of spending that kind of money on their political future. Greg advised the board that this one would need to go to a public plebiscite. The board accepted the challenge and embraced this as an opportunity to check the community pulse and to test the public support for a mandate to move this school system into the 21st century.

The road trips were arduous, the long hours were exacting and the debate was endless. Not since the last threat to change the paintwork on the school buses was there so much interest in the education system. The leadership team took the plan to every member of the school staff and pleaded for support – challenging staff to talk to their neighbors about the value for kids. The team talked to parent meetings in every community. Most communities seemed supportive, a few were non-committal. One community actively organized to campaign against the plebiscite. The board saw benefit in the campaign because it served to raise issues and bring balance to the discussion, and it seemed to strengthen the support for technology. Greg and Will tried to stay out of the debate, while at the same time speaking persuasively to key personnel in the district about the opportunities that the technology plan would present to student learning. Skeptics used these "new learning opportunities" as fuel to demonstrate that the world was going to hell in a hand basket, "After all, can you imagine how many teachers we could hire with money that's being wasted on this passing fancy!" said some. The tech coordinator stubbornly defended the infrastructure decisions; the assistant superintendent freely cited the educational advantages; the superintendent spoke of relevant growth opportunities; and the board chair touted the virtues of equal opportunity for all students.

When all was said and done, the public bought it, the plebiscite passed with a resounding majority and the plan was under way. It was no surprise that a few of the small communities had failed to support the venture; however, their paucity of votes carried no weight. Antelope Range was poised to enter the technology age!

Developing strategies for technology implementation

Fortunately Greg and Will had carefully structured the budget to acknowledge research and development, professional development and training. This forced the technology coordinator to work within the budget and to spend on targeted resources only, rather than on gadgets, toys and other wizardry. Contracts were signed, technician staff hired and a new technological language was adopted. People chatted about bytes and bits, kilobytes and gigabytes, microwave and broad bands, and WANs and LANs. The education community talked about computer-friendly classrooms, about integrating technology into the curriculum, distance education, computer-supported instruction and computer-delivered instruction. All the while there were those who claimed that technology would cost some teachers their jobs, that students

would be denied a "basics" education, and that computers would do nothing for special education.

Greg and Will relentlessly pursued their principals to promote the teaching and learning dialogue in the schools. They structured a series of teacher workshops to explore teaching pedagogy enhanced with technology, and they challenged all staff to get involved. They knew that adopter-adapter theory suggested that there would be some reluctance and resistance, but they pushed ahead. At teachers' urging they identified key professional development experiences for interested staff.

Will tapped into networks of technology folk right across the province. Interest and moral support emanated from other school systems. Sales personnel were only too anxious to display their products. The Department of Learning also became involved, staking its claim on the distance delivery project. Partnerships were formed and more contracts negotiated. Antelope Range was high stepping through an exciting movement, albeit a potential minefield!

Developing the stop-checks

Throughout all the excitement Greg had to ensure that communication and reporting requirements were diligently implemented. The coordinator was constantly under pressure to provide updates to Will, to Greg, the board and to the principals' group. Discussions were frequently spirited and questions abounded. Problem-solving was constant!

The regular business of the school system proceeded in consort with the technology initiative. The teaching quality project, special education programs, early literacy and English as a Second Language initiatives were all being launched simultaneously. Consultation and committees became an essential part of the Antelope Range culture. It became evident that the board had now moved into a new comfort zone. It was a zone that prioritized policy making and new program initiatives. While this created Greg and Will the space that they needed to effectively do their leadership work, it also meant that reporting became a way of life. Meetings, discussion, dialogue and consultation characterized the Antelope Range enterprise. The technology plan also triggered an unprecedented emphasis on planning. Plans were developed for building, capital expenditure, operations, maintenance programs, efficient transportation and small school survival. With all of this activity, a serious challenge emerged for Greg. There was a distinct danger that each of these projects could fracture the system, that each project could create a silo effect, that each project could develop a life of its own, unaware of the "big picture." Greg's next challenge was to connect all of this activity in a meaningful way. The common thread needed to be front and centre in all of the dialogue.

Intentions versus tensions

The "ante" in Antelope Range had certainly gone up, so to speak. Teachers were feeling pressure. Clearly, in the span of a few years they had been shaken from their complacency. Belief statements, technology plans, programs to address individual needs and new understandings about professionalism were all calling for commitment, new levels of dedication and leadership. Nowhere was this pressure felt more than in the principal ranks. The advent of new programs brought with it new expectations of accountability. It seemed that site-based decision-making wasn't so "site-based" after all! The common system-wide programs meant more shared decisions, more accountability and – more work.

Will needed to prepare a report for the principals and the board reflecting the extent to which schools were prepared for the implementation of the Integrated and Communication Technology (ICT) curriculum. The advent of the technology framework meant that Antelope Range was now equipped to manage the program. The system inventory revealed that schools were well stocked with modern computers and the high-speed infrastructure had recently come on stream. When Will surveyed the staff to explore the level of preparation he was shocked at the responses. Generally his survey found:

● 60% of the teaching staff was not confident that they could implement the curriculum. They were asking for training in mostly *basic skills*.

● 90% of staff claimed not to understand how to integrate technology into their teaching.

● 90% of staff was unaware how technology might enhance their teaching.

● 50% of staff expressed reluctance to change their way of teaching, even with more professional development and training.

These results acted as a wake-up call to the leadership team. Greg and Will went to their principals with this data and sought advice. The ICT curriculum was scheduled for mandatory implementation the next year and even with the equipment and infrastructure in place it seemed that Antelope Range was not ready. It was back to committee work. Will called on the technology coordinator to form a task force made up of lead teachers (those who understood the potential of technology in the classroom), and to generate some strategies to implement the curriculum effectively. As it evolved, it turned out that this committee provided the blueprint that Will needed. The committee's recommendations included:

1. Divert some Research and Development funds to provide basic training workshops and enhanced professional development for staff;

2. Establish a model classroom to demonstrate technology enhanced teaching and learning;

3. Develop a planning template for each school to map out the ICT curriculum outcomes by grade level, showing each teacher's responsibilities and a timeline for implementation.

This three-pronged plan of attack provided the vehicle to take the plan forward. The important component was that the lead teacher from each school was now linked very tightly with the implementation process. This had an immediate positive effect. Principals up until now had been expected to do the heavy lifting of implementation – and it simply wasn't happening. Greg discovered that the shared leadership model was clearly advantageous for this type of work (Joyce, Calhoun & Hopkins, 1999; Lambert, 1998). It afforded ownership while building a capacity within the system to support new initiatives. Another clear advantage with this approach was the opportunity to link the leadership process with learning (Caldwell, 2002).

Greg and Will pulled the resources together to establish the model classroom (see No. 2 committee recommendation). The teacher selected for the project had full responsibility to research, equip and design her classroom. Her training and preparation were all geared to using a constructivist approach to teaching. This model class was to be built on inquiry-based learning – a major departure from a culture that had a long history of teacher-centered learning. When the classroom came on stream, Antelope Range teachers could apply to spend a week in the demonstration room, with a colleague, observing and participating in the constructivist way of doing things, and exploring the potential of the technology. Using this approach, Will was able to provide hands-on professional learning for those teachers who volunteered to go through the program. Next, the teachers who went through the program established study groups in their own schools to share their understanding, to research ways to apply their learning in their own school and to develop implementation plans. These teachers also formed a study group with their colleagues from other schools who had gone through the program as a forum for further ongoing support. Growth and nurturing are fostered in a herd environment and don't survive in isolation.

Keys to successful technology implementation

Greg had learned that implementation strategy needed to be carefully developed and monitored. A key to the success of this process was the distributed leadership aspect. Through this, Greg was able to develop shared purpose, ownership and common understanding. The program no longer felt and looked like a top-down imposition. People on staff could now take responsibility for their own learning. They had a structure through which, as a staff, they could implement the new curriculum, take ownership for their professional development, open a dialogue with other staff and tap into the resources needed to make changes in their classrooms. They became energized as they realized the opportunities for inquiry and innovation.

Now there was a direct three-way link among leadership, the technology plan and student learning. In the meantime the workshop focus had been re-designed such that basic technology skills could be accessed on demand in pre-packaged, certificated, skill clusters. Teachers appreciated the opportunity to take these modules on their own time and at their own pace, and the results were encouraging. The teacher support initiative was re-focused to include

local expertise in mentoring arrangements, limited visits to outside schools and continued support for the study groups. The scope and sequence work was done at the school level with the principal collaborating with staff to blueprint the ICT curriculum implementation in a three-year staged plan. Greg and Will had carefully shifted responsibility for change into the teachers' domain. Now there was less panic, less resistance and more cooperation as teachers acknowledged the support and responded to their professional challenges.

Greg reflected on the conditions and changes that had been made to accommodate the planning and implementation of the technology plan. The district had established:

1. incentives for teacher inquiry

2. opportunity for teacher inquiry

3. teacher capacity for leadership in innovation and inquiry

4. respect for teacher authority

5. flexible school structure

6. responsive and supportive administration

7. sufficient time

8. sufficient resources, and

9. regulatory flexibility (Ancess, 2000).

Antelope Range was beginning to function as a professional learning community.

Workshop Questions:

1. Is your district's technology plan addressing intended outcomes that are defensible, sustainable and purposefully linked to learning?

   Ideally a committee will take on these questions, but teachers need to be full partners in the discussion. Are the outcomes clearly identified and positioned with a scope and sequence? Are the outcomes measured and reported? Are there provisions for flexibility to capture the needs of the students and the strengths of the teaching staff?

2. How can you ensure that technology becomes a tool for learning in your school?

   The "ensure" part of this question is the key to professional learning community. Reflection and dialogue needs to be supported by substantial data, inquiry and sustained focus.

3. Is your support infrastructure robust enough to support learning in a technologically friendly setting?

Are connectivity, transmission of data, hardware and software, and human resources meeting an acceptable standard? Technicians and lead teachers need to work together on these questions. Connecting with current standards and emerging learning needs should inform this dialogue.

4. How many of your staff are adopters, adapters or resisters? Why are they taking these stances?

This is tricky work! Leaders should be immersed in the initiatives sufficiently to be able to identify which staff members belong to which category. The key to this question is how to follow up on the data. What strategies are we adopting to support our adopters and adapters? Is there a consistent effort to provide staff with the skills and tools that they need for the job? What resources are being gainfully employed to provide and track results of professional and technical improvement efforts?

> *"Communities of the mind are collections of individuals who are bonded together by natural will and to a set of shared ideas and ideals."*
>
> *Thomas Sergiovanni*

Chapter Four

Focusing on New Professionalism

Is our commitment to staff development and professional growth consistent with our expectations and goals?

"Ground Zero"

Greg's immediate agenda when he was first appointed as superintendent for Antelope Range did not include attending to matters of professional practice in the schools. He had to focus on building some sound infrastructure and order to the system. However, he was well aware that the important work of teaching and learning would ultimately become the focus of his energy and the key to moving the system along the path to effectiveness (Hord, 1997a). The district was unlikely to grow and develop unless there were substantial elements of the professional learning community being practiced.

As Greg immersed himself in developing the supporting structure for the system, he was able to observe the attitudes and dispositions toward professional practice. What he observed was essentially a system without a structure. Matters of teaching competency were superficially addressed by a cyclical evaluation process that was inherited from days gone by. Essentially, the principal or somebody from central office evaluated the teachers on a once-every-three (or five)-years basis. The central office personnel usually evaluated new teachers eligible for tenure.

Professional development did not appear to be central to teachers' lives – it was either sporadic and disconnected at best, or an imposition at worst. A few teachers attended some conferences and workshops;

all teachers participated in their two-day convention; and school "PD" days seemed to be regarded as some kind of "rite of passage" but certainly not as a vehicle for staff development. Greg didn't notice any unifying threads to the professional development activity; much of the pursuits didn't conform to any larger purpose – most had to do with what to do on Monday morning. There was no structure in place to share the learning, and very few teachers were able to tap into financial support for professional development.

When Greg hired Will, he gave him prime responsibility to get a handle on the professional practice and to develop appropriate policies to facilitate professional growth within the system. Will surveyed and interviewed the staff to determine his starting point. He was anxious to determine motivation, perspectives and opportunities for professional growth, and the extent to which teachers received support in analyzing their teaching practice. The results of this exercise provided Will with a starting point. These were the key findings:

- The cyclical evaluation process was only sporadically implemented. Some staff were never evaluated.

- There was no common instrument to observe teaching practice.

- Written reports were generally awash with flattering rhetoric and platitudes, and rarely described the quality and attributes of the teaching.

● The cyclical evaluation process did not comply with recent legislation that governed supervision practice.

● Funding for an individual's professional development was either unavailable or arbitrarily assigned to a few teachers, and certainly not connected to any criteria.

● School "PD" days usually were, at best, spent on routine planning activity; at worst, on low-level questionable professional needs such as "rest and recuperation" or "tidying up." Not one teacher cited any purpose, direction or goals that might guide professional growth decisions.

● "Blaming" behavior prevailed. When asked to offer reasons for the poor state of PD, teachers blamed principals and central office, principals blamed teachers and central office, and central office people threw their hands in the air claiming that site-based decision-making was at the root of the problem.

Will found that understanding this data was not a major challenge, and drawing conclusions was even less of a problem. This was a deplorable state of affairs. Something needed to be done!

Responding to community expectations and partnering

Will began by weighing what he now knew. The new legislation clearly emphasized teachers taking professional responsibility for their learning (Alberta Learning, 1998). It also stressed an ongoing approach to supervision practice rather than a cyclical once-in-a-while practice. He also knew that the Antelope Range public, and particularly parents and students, had routinely expressed concerns about the quality of teaching in the district. He balanced this information with the directive that Greg had put on his lap to implement some policy to address these issues.

Will decided that his committee for this project would most appropriately be the principals' group. It seemed that this group was central to implementing changes in the supervision, growth and evaluation practices in Antelope Range. Although the group did

not embrace the prospect of working on this committee, Will solicited the help of a few principals to assist him in drafting a new policy. What followed was pivotal to the continued growth and development in Antelope Range. The small committee partnered with teachers, the professional association and the Department of Learning to check the perspectives of those with vested interests. Conflicting views prevailed. The Minister of Education had collaboratively established new legislation that acknowledged the professional status of the teacher, but, at the same time, he had included very specific standards to guide teaching practice – in fact, these standards were not guidelines – they were legislated expectations. The professional association interpreted the legislation as a license for teachers to be freed from oppressive, archaic and unfair forms of evaluation – but, at the same time, they were also freed to make decisions to attend to their own professional growth. Teachers, too, expressed the view the new act had allowed them to break the bonds of dependency, so they simply wanted to be left alone! What to do?

Developing systemic policy to support growth, supervision and evaluation

Will's committee came back to the principals' group with a policy draft that cut across the middle ground. It addressed the principal's responsibilities for ongoing supervision practice; it provided a means to facilitate teacher growth; it outlined how and when to evaluate teacher practice; and it required principals to report on supervision activity. The last part of this policy got everybody's attention. Reporting cut right to the heart of accountability. When several of the principals resisted this requirement, the debate centered on not only the public's right to be assured of competent teaching practice, but its right to be informed of such practice. After extensive discussion and consultation on this issue, the draft policy remained intact. The board was convinced that principals were the linchpin to creating a culture that valued good teaching practice, and that they were indeed accountable to do so!

The draft policy also tackled roles and responsibilities regarding teacher growth. It called for teachers to annually file and update their plan for personal growth. Again territorial issues were central to the debate. Principals were adamant that the Teacher Professional Growth Plan (TPGP) content remain between the teacher and the principal. It was not a matter for "reporting." Greg, Will and the board finally agreed to compromise on this one in the interest of collaboration and to salvage the key content of the policy. But, in fact, the content of some TPGPs did indeed become very contentious at a later time in Antelope Range (see later in this chapter).

Once these issues were settled, the board adopted the policy. However, it did so accompanied by a strong word of caution by the Board Chairperson, who was sensitive to public opinion. He reminded Greg that the principal's role was crucial in successfully implementing this policy, that leadership inferred a public trust and that the board needed assurance regarding the continued competency and growth of its teachers.

The next challenge was to change the culture from evaluation (such as it was) to supervision of the professional community.*

Supporting the professional practice

Principals expressed concern about the requirement to report on their supervision practice. This raised two very important issues. First, principals questioned why Antelope Range needed a detailed description of the scope of the supervision activity. Will chose to tackle this problem by constantly referring to the accountability that accompanies empowered leadership. He also provided specific guidelines for the principals' supervision reports. The details of the guidelines provided direction for:

● monitoring TPGPs

● observing teaching practice

● dialoguing about teaching

● investigating parent or student complaints about teaching

● making a decision to move a teacher into formal evaluation mode

Second, Will was pressed by many of his teachers to explain the meaning of the standards and to provide guidelines for interpreting the Education Minister's standards for teaching. It seemed that teachers were asking for clarification about the criteria for good teaching practice and how these criteria were to be applied. This was a much trickier problem! Several, if not all, the principals claimed that the teaching standards were sufficient as they stood. But when Will pressed them to describe what teaching would look like if a principal had concerns and needed to move the teacher into formal evaluation, the discussion ground to a halt. Making these judgments was difficult when standards were subjective, and was doubly difficult when no two people agreed on how to interpret the difference between a standard being met and one that wasn't. Will solicited Greg's help to flush out an understanding and interpreting of the teaching standards.

The challenging question became, "How do we describe the teaching standards in performance language?" "What does competency look like?" "What does marginal performance look like?" Greg and Will decided to analyze each of teaching standards and draw on their years of teaching experience to describe four levels of performance for each standard. The result was a four-level rubric that provided a clear understanding of competency levels and gave teachers and principals a tool for assisting in the evaluation process. The analytic nature of the rubric would enable teachers and evaluators to pinpoint strengths and weaknesses to provide a basis for improved practice (see Appendix C).

Teaching practice made accountable? An outrage!

This instrument sent a lightning bolt right across Antelope Range! Teachers were outraged that somebody other than themselves would make judgments about their teaching. Some principals claimed they couldn't understand the language contained in the

---

*Shirley Hord (1997) is attributed with defining and clarifying professional community as a collaborative, enquiry-based, goal-driven, dialogue-sustained enterprise. Leithwood et al. (1999) state that norms, beliefs, values and widely shared assumptions are rarely formed and changed in a direct way. "People do not change their values…by simply being told that they should" (p. 82). He further contends that culture change is a product of repeated experiences over a lengthy period of time combined with both implicit and explicit reflection.

rubric.* Others thought that a rubric describing teaching practice was hardly a professional tool-rubrics were only designed to make judgments about student performance! Yet others expressed the view that a holistic rubric would serve the purpose better than an analytic one because it wouldn't be as insulting! The holistic approach would provide an overall perspective of the teaching rather than the analytic, detailed exposure of the various components of the teacher's practice. To some it was insulting to acknowledge that some aspects of teaching practice might not meet a standard. When Greg and Will sifted through all the resistance it became clear that the teaching rubric was intimidating to some teachers. The potential of the tool to act as a device to compare their teaching to a standard was threatening, to say the least.

Greg and Will took the concerns to the office of the Minister of Education. The Minister' officials responded that this type of work was exactly what was intended when the minister created the Teaching Quality Standard, and advised Antelope Range to stay the course. Further, the minister's people asked that the rubrics be made available to other school systems as a model for how to interpret the standards for teaching. The Provincial Teaching Association was less than enamored with the rubric, but they reluctantly agreed that the criteria used to judge that a teacher might need to improve needed to be spelled out, clearly understood and consistent with the Teaching Quality Standards.

Will suspected that the flurry of resistance to the teaching standards might also be a sign of another problem – a lack in effective leadership in the district. Greg had expected his principals to act as vital facilitators in implementing the vision and goals in Antelope Range. This called upon complex leadership skills – skills that were apparently lacking with the Antelope Range principals. Principals were expected to help construct a shared vision, to facilitate dialogue with a student learning focus, to promote distributed leadership, to participate in collaborative processes, to structure the relevant questions and to develop and clarify the problems of practice. All of these skills were necessary to implement the supervision, growth and evaluation policy. Principals who were possibly intimidated by the magnitude of these expectations were initiating much of the resistance to the policy. With this in mind, Greg and Will determined it was time to solicit some outside assistance to develop a leadership development project (see Professor Rhodes, Chapter Three).

An interesting aside in this discussion was that a few teachers had stepped up to support the movement. They embraced the opportunity to use performance descriptors to reflect on their teaching, and they welcomed a system that would encourage and support a focus on improvement.

Developing the common language – again

The resistance to the performance level work died down once it became clear that the minister's office endorsed the work, that the teacher's association wasn't prepared to be seen taking a stance "against" teaching competency and that neither Greg nor Will was prepared to compromise student learning. With minor modifications the principals eventually endorsed the rubrics and, yet again, a new language was born. Teachers and administrators now had a way of using a "clearly-understood" common language to describe teaching practice. Although some were never comfortable with the idea that their performance was being "rated," the rubrics fast became a means of brokering the dialogue about teaching practice in Antelope Range. Teachers were able to look at the rubric and self-assess and reflect – practices that were strongly encouraged in the professional growth policy. Some used the language of the rubric as a way to open a conversation with colleagues and to share ideas without fear of reprisal. A few teachers found that their performance on the rubric directed their growth in some key areas of teaching. Supervisors and evaluators were able to pinpoint areas of strength and weakness for beginning teachers and to guide growth and development. Teachers who did not understand the deeper meaning of words such as "decontextualized" and

---

*A rubric is a vehicle used to guide human judgement. Specifically, it consists of a fixed scale of values or characteristics along with performance levels describing the characteristics. See Appendix C.

"pedagogical practice" continued to allow their dander to be raised but, despite the rocky beginnings, the rubrics had prevailed!

Directing the resources and energies

Teacher Professional Growth Plans (TPGP) did not necessarily enjoy the same success as did the rubrics describing teaching performance. The problems with the TPGPs were threefold: first, the policy made an assumption regarding the teacher's motivation, skills and professional commitment; second, school principals were expected to bring facilitating skills to the table when reviewing TPGPs; and third, to be effective, growth plans needed somehow to link with school and system goals, with student learning needs and with the teacher's performance on the teaching quality rubric. This was a tall order – a lot to expect! Perhaps the effectiveness of the growth plans was summed up when one Antelope Range teacher proudly shared with her colleagues, "I'm using my growth plan to learn how to speak Portuguese!" On the surface, this might have sounded very profound. However, since there wasn't a Portuguese program offered in Antelope Range (or anywhere in the province for that matter), and neither was this teacher ever likely to be assigned a Portuguese teaching job, Greg concluded that the TPGP program in Antelope Range could be in trouble. Certainly people were free to learn Portuguese, but as a professional growth plan? Hardly! Somebody had dropped the ball.

Assessing the progress

The journey to create a culture that makes teaching and learning a priority is an arduous one, and Antelope Range had only just begun. But Greg was able to report good progress to the board. The board had passed the enabling policy. Greg had created guidelines – by developing monitoring procedures, establishing standards of performance and identifying opportunities for growth. All of the organizational structure to support sustainable change was in place.

Still, the first round of principals' reports on their supervision practice did not indicate that the profile of this policy was particularly high. Some of the reports were superficial, indicating only marginal activity, while a few others showed signs of promise.

Will summarized the reports for the board. Principals' supervision practice revealed:

● Principals were satisfied with teacher competency;

● Teachers were lukewarm in their response to the teacher growth plan policy;

● Limited programs were implemented to respond to emerging student needs;

● There were some efforts to focus on learning about technology-based teaching;

● Student assessment practices continued to be based on traditional testing only.

The dialogue with principals about what these reports were saying revealed that some had perhaps not understood what was expected. However, only one principal asked for an opportunity to prepare another report to provide a clearer picture of her supervision practice. Greg and Will realized that this first experience could be regarded as part of a learning experience, but, without further attention, it could also prove to be a limiting factor in this school system's growth and development. Greg and Will were beginning to grasp the meaning of patience. Years of apathy meant that progress was slow and difficult, especially with only limited opportunities to change the personnel. The follow-up discussion with the board and the principals about the reports had served notice about accountability if nothing else.

On the positive side there were only limited cited instances of marginally competent teaching, and in those cases the policy was serving its purpose. A few teachers were already working on improvement plans and in those instances the principal and teacher had collaboratively designed the improvement plan and were working on improving performance. Parent concerns about teaching were receiving an improved systematic level of response from both principals and teachers. And some teachers were stepping forward and expressing willingness to participate in the technology-model learning program. Greg and Will thought it timely to build on the beginnings and to facilitate a sustainable growth process.

Raising the ante

Greg and Will boldly outlined a strategy to move the growth activity to the next level. They acknowledged two important goals – both intended to provide stimulus for the activity: to provide supports for teacher professional growth and to encourage a focus on purposefully linking teacher growth to system-wide initiatives. They did this by carefully structuring a number of partnerships to support teacher growth. In some instances new funding was established to support professional development activity directly linked to TPGPs; in others matching fund incentives were provided to support growth in areas pertaining to school, district and province-wide goals; and in yet others, grants were established to support innovative teaching practice that enhanced learning through technology, literacy and special education.

Summary

Antelope Range had taken several steps toward creating professional learning community. Most of the support came in the form of funding, incentive grants, modeling and focusing on competency standards. Subsequently there was a heightened awareness regarding professional obligations, but there was an accompanying reaction to this direction. Issues came to the fore as teachers felt that they were subject to new burdens of accountability. It would appear that the foundation work for establishing a professional learning community would take continuous, ongoing effort. But the initial steps had been taken!

Workshop Questions:

1. To what extent does our district structure its use of time and resources to support instructional goals and priorities?

2. How does professional development support – or fail to support – our systemic goals, objectives and instructional priorities?

3. To what extent do we use one-off staff development sessions without appropriate follow-up and staff support to institutionalize change elements?

4. How do we use – or fail to use – best practices in staff development, including: peer coaching, study groups, job-embedded practice and action research to focus on effective teaching and learning?

> *"The most promising strategy for sustained, substantive school improvement is developing the ability of school personnel to function as professional learning communities."*
>
> *Dufour & Eaker, 1998, p. xi*

Chapter Five

Leadership, Planning and Reporting

Are our accountability processes aligned to our goals and priorities?

The planning process: Goals, objectives and priorities

Greg, in discussion with his board, thought it particularly important to design strategies to address the sustainability challenges implicit in the new Antelope Range initiatives – shared decision making, technology and professionalizing teaching. He knew that meaningful and effective long- and short-term planning were imperative to align resources with the intentions of the system. He also knew that purposeful planning and reporting were required not only by the province, but the process provided an opportunity to collectively focus on the goals of the district. But planning in itself wouldn't necessarily help connect the various projects and initiatives to the common purpose. There was a distinct danger, for example, that if teacher growth plans, grants for innovative classroom projects and support for professional development were not purposefully linked, these initiatives could easily run out of steam. On the up side, if links were constantly established and interconnectivity were to permeate the planning and reporting, then each of the projects would indeed be enhanced and strengthened by the collective force of mutual supports (Bamburg & Andrews, 1990; Fullan, 1997; Leithwood, 1995).

Once again, Greg and Will turned their attention to the one element that lay at the heart of success or failure for any of the Antelope Range projects that could facilitate the linkage strategies – leadership. They began by teasing out the common understandings about leadership and by looking at the data revealed in the leadership survey intended to inform Professor Rhodes' work. The limited data on the leadership capacity in the system revealed:

● Most people in the school system viewed leadership as a domain manifested by one individual (i.e., the principal or the superintendent). There was little acknowledgement that leadership could be shared or distributed in any significant way.

● Leadership was generally regarded as a support endeavor for teachers. Effective leadership meant helping teachers solve problems, managing student discipline cases and keeping parents happy – and out of the way.

● Few acknowledged the connection between leadership and accountability for student achievement.

● When pressed, staff members were unable to articulate goals and directions for the school or the system.

● People generally regarded the decision-making processes as a form of "dumping on the schools" by the government and the school board.

To address this issue of connected, purposeful activity, Greg coupled the focus on leadership with a decision to restructure the planning processes used in the district. He outlined a structure that called for inextricably linking government, school board and school plans. Previous to this the Antelope Range schools had been left to their own devices to create plans. Although the plans had been "required," there had been no monitoring, follow up and reporting procedures to place the planning process within an overall context.

Again Greg began with a draft policy. His draft contained:

1. A planning cycle
2. An integrated process connecting resource allocation to planning, and planning with results
3. Reporting the results
4. Establishing targets
5. Formulating plans to meet student needs
6. Connecting planning process with the site-based decision-making policy.

The principals felt more than a little overwhelmed by the scope of this policy. Given their record with respect to reporting on their supervision practice, it was no surprise that again, their major hang-up was the reporting phase. The issue of trust was trotted out: "Can't you just trust that we'll do it?" The issue of workload emerged in the discussion: "Isn't planning another make-work and paper-work imposition?" And the issue of flexibility was raised: "My plans change from day-to-day so that I can respond to the needs of my students!" These and other manifestations of resistance convinced Greg that he was touching a nerve. The problem was clear: Holding people accountable for results caused stress and anxiety. However, Greg could see no other way to challenge his staff to take plans seriously and to encourage full participation in pursuit of goals. The Education Department's policy on setting targets and reporting the results was quite clear. One of the purposes of the student achievement testing program was to provide data with a view to improving the program.*

Setting targets – analysis and reflection

The idea of beginning planning by setting student achievement targets was a difficult sell. Greg had to convince his principals that all planning, all school improvement practices, all professional growth and so forth, had to begin with identifying the desired outcomes. He emphasized that learning and achievement targets established the bar, provided a means for aligning resources and gave impetus to the planning activity for the school district. Once again there were those who resisted this focus on the grounds that target setting was a meaningless, arbitrary and perhaps theoretical process that was in no way grounded in the realities of the classroom. Classes were different from one year to the next, curriculum changed, student needs were in a state of flux, caring and relationships were more important than achievement levels and a variety of other excuses were offered in an attempt to avoid setting targets and being held accountable for reaching those targets. Greg acknowledged his principals' concerns. He suggested that perhaps they could broaden the discussion on this issue by going back to the board and public to check for understanding and perceptions about the integrity of learning and achievement in the Antelope Range belief statements. The principals declined this invitation. (Greg's groundbreaking work in creating infrastructure was starting to pay off!)

And so it was that the exercise of setting achievement targets became the first step in the Antelope Range planning process. The policy called for this target-setting process to be informed by a thorough examination of the individual, school and district results – recent achievement results, principals' supervision reports and the district satisfaction survey results. Greg explained to his principals that this meant "unpacking" the relevant school data to enhance a thorough understanding of the context.

*Policies 2.1.1 through 2.1.6 represent the accountability process for [the province's] public and separate schools, and funded private schools. These policies detail requirements for school authorities re: planning and reporting; teacher evaluation; student evaluation; use and reporting of results on provincial assessments; and on financial accountability and audits as required by provincial statutes, regulations and policies. (Policy, Regulations, and Forms Manual, Accountability in Education, Revised Feb. 1997)

Table 1: Antelope Range Planning Cycle

Month	Planning Activity
January	Identify achievement targets, new programs.
February	Preliminary budget submissions from school and support sites (goals, budgets and enrolment projections).
March	Preliminary district budget distributed to school and support sites.
April	Board hearings, submissions. Review satisfaction survey data.
May	Complete long-range (three-year) plans. Final budget submission to government.
June	Develop school "program and services blueprints" and report these to the board.
July/August	Final allotment of resources to school and support sites.
September	Enrollment reports – adjustments. Exam results reports analysis.
October	Final school and district results reports to board and province.
November	Community-board meetings (Review results, identify issues).
December	Auditor's report.

It soon became apparent that this planning policy was going to drive a continual ongoing cycle of activities that would link planning to the important foci of the district. The Planning Cycle also made it clear that thorough planning was staged and ongoing (see Table 1).

Linking accountability and growth

The next step was to create a clear understanding that the planning process needed to be open, transparent and responsive. Greg built in time and opportunities for consultation, and collaboration such that each school and support site could identify its own issues and make submissions to the district plan. He also established clear expectations for reporting – when, what and how. He carefully planned some workshops to promote the skills the principals needed to carry out these functions. These communication expectations and procedures implicitly created a culture about effective planning, but explicitly outlined the expectations for accountability. Greg cited the provincial reporting structure as a model for what he expected:

> The provincial planning cycle and accountability framework assume a collective and reciprocal professional and personal responsibility for the continuous improvement of performance. If the planning loop is incomplete, provincial planning occurs in a vacuum. The perception appears to be that jurisdiction priorities must fit within provincial goals when in fact provincial priorities are most effectively abstracted from jurisdiction reports. (Burger et al., 2001)

For example the schools and the district both were provided a template for reporting student achievement results. This structure required that targets were identified along with the results, and a

Table 2: Antelope Range Sample Student Achievement Report (Grade 9) 2000-2001

Course	Achievement Target	Number of Students	% of Students Meeting Target
Math	90% will pass 15% will excel	275	83% 22%
Language	95% will pass 20% will excel	275	91% 25%
Science	90% will pass 20% will excel	286	83% 18%
Social Science	95% will pass 20% will excel	286	89% 23%

mechanism for reporting on the targets being met and not met was included.

Another component of the reporting progress included an anecdotal accounting of activity relating to the district school improvement goals. Greg stressed that this form was intended as a tool to report real evidence, and not extraneous unrelated material (see Figure 2).

These planning and reporting efforts went a long way toward clearly establishing what was important in

Figure 2. Report on Improvement Goal Number 1

(Provide quality technologically-supported learning experiences for all students)

School:_____

Goal:_____
_____
_____

Initiatives: (List program initiatives to support this goal)

1._____
2._____
3._____

Results: (Provide quantitative and qualitative evidence of activity. Schools may include artifacts to support these results)

1._____
2._____
3._____

Professional Development: (List the teacher growth activity, e.g., research, TPGPs, peer interaction, workshops, conferences, etc., in support of this goal)

_____
_____
_____
_____

Antelope Range. The implementation part of the process was still at issue – it required careful monitoring, support and skillful facilitation. And this was, at least in part, why Professor Rhodes was contracted to work with the principals.

Rhodes' work had only marginal impact on the principals (reported previously in Chapter Three). Few of them responded to the challenge to engage in ongoing site-based follow-up activity, and the whole group sessions quietly ran their course, then disappeared. However, Greg recognized that this work was not without some positive indicators: it enhanced the district-wide expectation that leadership was central to growth and development; it raised issues of commitment and team-player capability; and it exposed some gaping holes between plans and actual day-to-day activity in the school system.

Greg soon realized he needed to force the issue with respect to the leadership required to support his planning policy. He responded with the only tool left at his disposal, the principal evaluation policy – the ultimate in accountability. It was only through this policy that Greg was able to effectively address issues of accountability. And when a few of the principals did not emerge successfully from the evaluation process, Greg knew that he finally had their attention.

Principal evaluation – a paradox

A serious paradox embedded in the nuances of assessing leadership and evaluating principals is that the two notions often get confused and intertwined. In Antelope Range, for example, principals were accountable for implementing policies, for planning practices, and for developing community and so on. On the other hand, a significant part of developing community was empowering participants to make decisions. It's conceivable that some of those empowered decision-makers could make poor decisions that potentially jeopardize the school or system results. And yet the principal evaluation policy ultimately held the principal's feet to the fire. Greg acknowledged this paradox by revising it to reflect a greater emphasis on *process*, rather than *functions*. It meant that some latitude could be created for accommodating some risk-taking, shared leadership and community building such that the full burden of getting results did not necessarily or solely rest on the princi-

pal's shoulders. What counted was how effectively had the principal empowered others, encouraged community involvement and built relationships such that the learning culture was improved. Now, participants in the evaluation process were judged more on a holistic basis, where the context became a key component of the evaluation. It was complex, but it moved the evaluation process away from checklist approaches to one of more effective reflective practice.

Although Greg acknowledged that leadership development was a priority that needed constant attention and nurturing, he also recognized that leadership was often the limiting factor in implementing change in Antelope Range. Some progress was evident and encouraging. Central office leadership in developing and implementing the technology plan had resulted in significant gains; teacher leadership in applying for and using innovation grants had resulted in some enquiry and project-based learning in classrooms; board members had demonstrated leadership in creating meaningful, enabling policy; and teacher professionalization work was being supported by some principals who were committed to improved practice and student achievement. These were encouraging signs.

All in all much had been accomplished. Greg knew that the effort needed to be an ongoing one for changes to be sustained. He thought it time to move to a more systemic and generic perspective and address some of the elements that were unique to his school district.

Workshop Questions:

1. How does your district allocate its resources? What are the budget steps or procedures in your district? Are there opportunities to respond to the unique aspects of your district? Who gets input into the budget development and under what circumstances?

2. To what extent does your district equitably distribute its resources to support clearly articulated systemic priorities and student achievement targets?

3. What are the primary sources of skepticism and cynicism within your district?

4. Are our long-range goals purposefully constructed to create meaning and direction for the resource-allocation and policies of the district? Do we monitor the evidence on our goals over a relatively long period of time?

5. Do our short-term objectives focus on the truly important goals that are directly related to teaching, learning and achievement?

6. To what extent is your district aligned in your collective understanding of shared vision, long-range goals and short-term objectives for staff performance and student achievement?

> *At the heart of sustained morale and motivation lie two ingredients that appear somewhat contradictory; on the one hand, positive attitudes toward the future and toward what one can accomplish through one's own intentional acts, and on the other hand, recognition that life is not easy and that nothing is ever finally safe.*
>
> *John Gardner, 1986, p. 10*

Chapter Six

Small Schools – Bane or Boom?

To what extent do cultural norms act as barriers to change, and can these norms be changed?

Greg had brought about a variety of serious change initiatives since assuming the superintendent's responsibilities in Antelope Range District #99. However, he wondered to what extent and how these changes were impacting on the classrooms around the district. He drew on the change theory advocates (Canadian Association of School Administrators, 1993; Day, Harris, Hadfield, Tolley & Beresford, 2000; Fullan, 1999, 2001b; Leithwood, 1995) and noted that he had followed much of the inclusive practices to ensure effective growth. He visited the culture group of authors (Barth, 2001; Deal & Peterson, 1999; Peterson & Deal, 2002; Sergiovanni, 2000) and understood that changing a culture is sometimes a slow and onerous process. Senge (1999) stated that in some ways clarifying a vision was easy. He thought a more difficult challenge lies in facing current reality. But Greg was convinced that there was something peculiar about Antelope Range that was influencing the rate of change and the extent to which school improvement was embraced in his district. He turned to Saphier and King (1985) to reflect on the 12 cultural norms that affect school improvement:

- Collegiality
- Experimentation
- High expectations
- Trust and confidence
- Tangible support
- Reaching out to viable knowledge bases
- Appreciation and recognition
- Caring, celebration and humor
- Involvement in decision-making
- Protection of what's important
- Traditions
- Honest, open communication

Whereas Greg acknowledged that checklists and formulas had limited application, he also mused that he had indeed attended to many of the cultural norms while trying to implement his changes. The Saphier and King (1985) model was supported by credible scientific research. But as he cast his eyes down the list he paused when he came to "protection of what's important" and "traditions." Could it be that he had overlooked something that might be contributing to the limited progress? He had not paid a lot of attention to community context from the perspective of its traditions, history and valued norms; and he had made assumptions that the community supported an improved standard in the quality of education.

Since Greg had assumed the key leadership position in Antelope Range, the profile of the school system had continued to depict a far-flung, remote, disparate geographic region comprising a series of small communities desperately clinging to their small schools. The population in the district was declining steadily. Industries (food processing, agriculture support and railways) had long since departed the area, leaving the farmers and ranchers to compete with the antelope for the spoils. But the spoils were sparse! Antelope Range boasted over 30 schools – but they were all small, ranging from 20 to 600 students, and most had fewer than 150 students.

Greg had adopted several strategies to gain support for his small school system, and to assure that there were adequate resources to operate school programs despite a paucity of student population. Among these measures were:

1. Compensatory funding. Greg's business operations staff had turned over all stones to access small school grants designed to compensate for the scarcity of his school communities. Greg had convinced the provincial authorities to acknowledge the scarcity challenges and as a result had acquired additional grants for schools, transportation, maintenance and administration.

2. Developmental grants. Greg had formed a partnership with the province to access capital funds designed to build the technology infrastructure. The installation of the Wide Area Network provided a high-speed backbone to enhance communication over long distances, and the government heavily supported this project.

3. Plebiscite. Greg had lobbied hard to win the approval and support of his electorate to fund a long-range technology plan. The positive vote had provided a solid base of continued financial support to replace computerized equipment on a cyclical basis.

4. Supplementary grants. Greg aggressively pursued every "strings attached" grant that would help his district. Language, literacy, technology and school improvement grants were examples.

5. Partnerships. The district had formed a partnership with a few other districts to deliver health services to students in need. Other contracts were entered into to provide support services and expertise that a small school district couldn't provide with its own staff.

When all things were considered Greg had considerably increased the supports available to his schools. The supplementary grants and programs meant that schools in his district were well-serviced and there was no shortage of money. This resulted in more opportunities for equity in the district. Regardless of the size of the school and regardless of its remote location, students had quality learning opportunities, a reasonable breadth of programs and a rich variety of support services.

Despite this Greg sensed that something was rotten in Denmark! He decided to pay attention to Saphier and King's (1985) cultural norms and to scratch the surface to find out what was beneath the apparent apathy. He brought in a data analyst and experienced educator to complete a thorough review of the history, the traditions and the underpinnings of the community. Much of the study was conducted by closely scrutinizing documents and artifacts – but a significant effort was made to talk to parents and students in the district. Once word got around that someone was asking questions, more and more people volunteered for interviews. There were a few focus group discussions but this time Greg avoided the lure of conducting another survey. First he felt that his people had been over-surveyed, and second, he was beginning to question the authenticity of some of the survey data that had emerged in the past. As it was, his contract team brought an abundance of "results" and "data" back to him by way of a report.

Small school syndromes and symptoms

Greg found that the twelve cultural norms from the Saphier and King (1985) list were indeed coming into play. The "culture" report revealed:

1. Dependency

2. Immunity

3. Suspicion

4. Distrust

For the first time Greg and Will were able to examine some rich information that was most profound. The history of the community revealed that many of the parents were only one and sometimes two generations from a time when the government had intervened in the area to assume title for farm land, which had the effect of sheltering the farmers during a devastating drought. The government then leased the land back to the farmers at an affordable rate. In addition much of the land became crown land that was then made available to the community as virtually free grazing land. This move had, in essence, saved the community from disaster. After that move, government was a very serious ongoing presence in the welfare of the community – strategically deploying offices and branches, providing employment and making services immediately available as needed.

This intervention, while providing a lifeline to the people, also had the effect of building up a dependence. It seemed that there was an underlying attitude throughout, that regardless of external economic conditions, the government would always be there for these people – and there was plenty of evidence to support that idea. The dependence spilled over into the education system and it manifested itself in two ways. First, the people in the community expected unlimited support for its schools regardless of the size of the school. If the students were few in number, the government was still expected to provide a program – and it usually did. This, in turn created very small classes, which sounds advantageous to students, but this wasn't necessarily the case. The small class sizes, instead, *contributed* to the dependence. Students expected lots of individual attention that translated into spoon-feeding. Students rarely had to think for themselves to resolve a problem because help was so close at hand, just as it had been for the grandparents who were helped by the government during the drought. A further spinoff from the dependence angle was that homework and study habits were both sadly lacking. Very few students conscientiously studied their course content outside of addressing some very basic homework requirements. Most thought that the teacher's final course review would be sufficient to prepare them for exams.

The immunity was a direct outgrowth from the dependency issues. Government grants and handouts had created a culture and expectations that help would always be around the corner if things got really bad. Apart from the positive effects that this had on sustaining the community and preserving the family farm, it also resulted in an attitude that results and production didn't really matter. The government would more often than not reinforce this scenario by obliging with a grant program to compensate for any shortage. This too spilled over into the school community, hence, the indifference in many cases about

results. Greg considered the achievement throughout the school system to fall far short of the potential. True, the achievement statistics seemed to indicate that the Antelope Range students were on a par, if not slightly better than the rest of the province. But when Greg considered the demographics of the district, he knew that achievement could be higher. For example, classes were small – that should have had a positive effect on results; schools weren't challenged by multi-cultural, multi-racial issues; resources were abundant; and special education needs were low. It seemed that Antelope Range, at least in part, suffered from complacency because there was a history of mediocrity and indifference about results.

This was also a community that over the years had declined and receded on the growth curves. Some people left the community; most young people would leave after school for jobs, leaving a few to live in the community. Very few new people moved into the community. This led to a comfort zone with traditional ways of doing things and an acceptance of tried and true practices. This certainly carried over into the school system, meaning that new methods were met with suspicion, skepticism and sometimes cynicism. Not hard to understand!

The same was true for leaders and teachers. If people who held these key positions were "from the outside" they were viewed with suspicion. Greg himself had been regarded as "fuzzy-headed" and "left wing" and full of "psycho-babble" as he wended his way and provided the guiding light through the minefield of change. Perhaps one parent summed up the distrust for people who were ostensibly from the outside when he questioned Will about a proposed new teaching method, "I ain't no Luddite, but I sure as heck can't understand why a kid would need to know how to use a computer to get an education!"

These were the contextual issues that were contributing to some of the resistance and reticence that Greg had been battling. Little wonder that changing a culture takes time. In this case Greg and Will were facing two generations of a social condition that was a very real influencing factor in the governance, the goal-setting and the accountability problems in the system. It was also a factor in student attitude.

Greg firmly believed that his students could reap the advantages of being educated in small schools. He believed that small schools:

- provided opportunities for close relationships that could benefit students in many ways;

- set students up for success because of low pupil teacher ratios;

- gave students and teachers better access to the learning resources;

- opened the doors for parents and community to form a close relationship with the school; and

- positioned the school as a source of pride in the community.

He was frustrated at the findings in the culture report, but, on the other hand, he was pleased that he had identified part of the problem. He wasn't willing to roll over, though. Now that he had some information about the history and traditions in the district, he could understand some reasons and rationale behind certain behaviors – but it didn't give him an excuse to give up!

Celebrating the culture

Instead of giving up – a thought that more than once crossed his mind – Greg took the opposite approach. He actively campaigned to celebrate the successes and opportunities for learners in his small schools. He did this in a two-prong approach. One was through a concerted effort to promote the positive opportunities in small schools by earmarking school improvement projects for his schools, and second, he went outside the school district to organize a network of support to celebrate small schools. Both of these initiatives generated much positive energy!

Workshop Questions:

1. Does your school system have differentiated funding structures to support small schools?

2. Describe the small school culture in your district. What is valued in these cultures? Do the small school results compare favorably to the district standards?

3. What is the history of small school closures in your district? Do the policies clearly outline the process? Are there opportunities built in for community input, and is the process consistent with the School Act?

> *"In order for the brain to comprehend, the heart must first listen."*
>
> *Perkins, 1992*

Chapter Seven

Reflecting and Learning

What are the lessons to be learned from honest and professional reflection?

Reflective practice is a valuable tool at both the teaching and at the leadership levels. In Greg's case he had taken an aggressive approach over the span of four or five years to centre his small rural education system on improved learning and accountability. The new programs and initiatives were all designed to either directly impact the learner or to support change toward that end. How could he know whether or not the changes were making a difference? Were the changes sustainable? Certainly he could measure increased activity; he could look at results, and he could examine satisfaction survey data. But each of these measures might not tell the whole story.... Greg knew that the changes had an abundance of breadth and scope, but did they have the depth such that they truly and positively affected student learning? To supplement the data analysis and to truly tap into the evidence of change, Greg opted for a think-tank approach. He convened his central office leadership team together with a school board member, a principal, and a teacher to review the district progress and to do a holistic check on the state of the union.

The task force convened over a few days in a retreat setting. A look at the hard data (student achievement and survey data) revealed only moderate improvement. The holistic overview was a little more encouraging, but it also exposed some harsh realities. The task force prepared a hard-hitting "cut to the chase" report card that provided Greg with what he needed to know.

Lessons learned

Lesson One. Greg thought that he had covered all the bases with the technology project but the impact did not match the energy and effort invested in the project. The technology project experienced only moderate success despite a) installing a high-speed infrastructure; b) addressing all the connectivity issues; c) planning for an abundant inventory of modernized equipment; d) drawing up timelines for curriculum implementation; and e) providing training and professional growth opportunities. Greg thought that he had assessed, addressed and provided for the new skills that staff might need, and he had allocated the time and resources for staff to learn these skills. He knew that this support was critically important in managing change. However, because the technology project was more about new and innovative ways of teaching than it was about technology, it wasn't easy to determine success. In retrospect the leadership team had not really given a great deal of thought to the way in which staff might actually acquire new teaching skills beyond arranging observation opportunities in the model classroom for staff. Greg thought that there would have been a better pay-off had he given more time and thought about the skills staff would need – how they would personally identify which skills they had and which they needed, and how they would then be supported in acquiring them. Also, the group study efforts that were designed to enhance the dialogue and support the professional learning community needed to embrace more participants rather than just those early adopters who were not afraid to tackle innovations. As it was, a great deal of time, energy and money was expended on the technology program with only marginal return in the student achievement domain. On the range, the herd was seemingly milling about but not heading off in any particular direction.

Lesson Two. The internal and external incentives, and resources, geared toward developing a professional learning community had resulted in some growth activity. Greg had a) guided professional growth by carefully diagnosing the results and examining the district profile to pinpoint targets for improvement; b) devised an action plan to provide support for focused workshops, seminars and conferences; c) encouraged peer and coaching relationships to support growth in targeted areas; and d) advocated for partnerships to provide alternative growth opportunities for teachers. Whilst each of these endeavors had resulted in more focused activity, there was still no evidence that there was a substantial change in classroom practice. Greg was left wondering about how to complete the loop. He was beginning to understand that beliefs, goals, aggressive supports and dialogue by themselves still did not guarantee success. There was something about the Antelope Range context that still needed to be interpreted and understood. The systematic nurturing had not necessarily resulted in a weaning process.

Lesson Three. The move toward accountability had not necessarily brought about a change in the culture. The discussion about understanding results and setting targets had encountered at worst a plethora of resistance and, at best, some superficial posturing. Greg had tried to create a culture that valued student learning above all else. He had stressed that teaching practices, if effective, must focus on student achievement and outcomes.

> Fundamental to an outcomes approach in education is a shift in focus from an emphasis on teaching and holding staff accountable for what they teach, to an emphasis on learning and holding staff accountable for what and how students learn. (Shortland Jones, 2002, p. 2)

In retrospect Greg thought that a meaningful move toward standards needed to engage more teachers in the discussion. He felt that this effort had been compromised by his principals' inability and reluctance to conduct the accompanying dialogue. The lesson here was that principals need to be not only strong communicators such that this dialogue can be facilitated, but they also need to be steeped in curriculum matters. If principals speak from a position of authority on teaching pedagogy, and have modeled their beliefs and understanding in this regard, they are much more likely to succeed in creating a culture that highly values student learning. If the leader of the pack has no understanding of the survival instincts, the pack is likely to dissipate though lack of purpose.

Lesson Four. Changing the culture is complex and, by nature, long-term. While a moderate cultural shift appeared to have occurred among the small group of teachers who participated in the initial two years of the technology project, the paucity of involvement by other staff pointed out a glaring flaw. This presented a conundrum! Greg understood that change incentive, persistence, shared values and ownership were all crucial components in the culture change process…and he had made some inroads in a few of these areas. But he had not succeeded in having a critical mass of teachers embrace change. Greg wondered to what extent he could promote continued change without massive large-scale incentives. Even then change is only skin deep without the personal commitment of the key players. You can lead a horse to water, but…!

Lesson Five. Change doesn't proceed exactly as planned. The planning and reporting processes had certainly brought focus to the school district. Principals had learned that empty rhetoric was no longer going to convince the board and the public that good things were necessarily occurring in their schools. Greg had certainly raised the stakes and introduced accountability into the process. However, plans, deadlines and reports in themselves are not enough to ensure change. Ongoing support and dialogue had not been sufficient to carry the change. The desired change needs to be embedded in daily practice and directly linked to the key components of the system. For example, teacher planning needs to be a topic of dialogue between teachers and principals; teacher growth plans need to guided by school and district goals; school plans need to closely align with district plans; results need to be carefully analyzed for relevance to targets; technology and other innovative efforts need to be judged in terms of their contribution to student achievement; and community collaboration needs to be focused on important matters that relate directly to learning. A certain amount of impetus can generate from concerted, coherent and purposefully linked activity, but a series of isolated, unrelated, individual efforts do nothing for systemic improvement! The survival instincts of the group as a whole through cooperation and pursuit of shared purpose are far stronger than isolated, parochial activity.

Lesson Six. It is sometimes convenient to focus on aspects that seem vital at the time but really are only tangential to the core business of the district. Greg had consciously focused first on stabilizing the management of the district, and second on building a governance infrastructure. Although these moves were necessary to provide a solid foundation for the district, they were not the reason for existence. Long after these projects were completed there were those who continually challenged, blamed and reacted to aspects of site-based and shared decision-making processes. It took a while for Greg to realize that this was just another variation of victim behavior – usually perpetrated by those who were disempowered by empowerment strategies, or who were intent on creating diversions from the important work at hand. Greg mused that leaders in a school system need to be clear about the directions and be able to refocus energies and resources to meet those ends. The whole domain of means and ends needed more attention. The blockers in the district were very adept at focusing on means rather than ends – and that is a never-ending exercise!

Lesson Seven. Attaining a shared understanding and collaboratively reaching clarity of vision is difficult and time consuming. Greg had learned that agendas ran rife in Antelope Range – and that he was not always successful in getting all the cards out on the table. When people are not mutually committed to open and honest dialogue, it is difficult to anticipate where the snakes lie in the grass. Many of the Antelope Range initiatives depended on cooperation, collaboration and professional integrity. These attributes can't be "bought" by offering incentives, they can't be counted on when there is a crisis and they can't be assumed to be present just because all the animals are at the same water trough.

Lesson Eight. Assessing students' achievement of outcomes, monitoring them and reporting them still remained a major challenge. Greg suspected that the reluctance to respond to the standards and accountability requirements was at least in part due to the perpetuation of outdated traditional assessment practices. He wondered how he could promote a shift toward fair assessment practice that included authentic assessment and an evidence-based approach to determining mastery of student learning. Many of his staff were locked into a traditional textbook-type assessment that only sporadically hit on curriculum outcomes. He believed that a renewed focus in this area might move teachers toward planning their teaching around curriculum-based learner outcomes.

Lesson Nine. Greg had managed to get a number of key components of change close to correct. He had built the infrastructure, provided a forum for discussion about purpose, and had vigorously supported positive change. The accountability efforts were stalled; the new program areas were only marginally implemented; and the professional growth and evaluation processes were essentially superficial. Greg knew that sustaining these initiatives would require persistence, commitment and focused leadership. Becoming impatient would likely take the district back to square one. Antelope didn't become the king of the range because there was sufficient grass on the home quarter – they had to move to find the greener pastures! Greg had to find other ways to stimulate growth.

Following this review, Greg, although somewhat disheartened, knew that for worthwhile change to endure in Antelope Range he needed to adopt some new strategies. The task force findings had demonstrated that change efforts were well-founded, strongly supported and purposefully targeted. But evidence equally strongly suggested that the changes were only superficial, and further, there were no indications that the culture had adjusted to sustain these changes over a period of time. Greg was beginning to comprehend that significant change in Antelope Range was going to require a renewed focus and a long-term initiative.

Greg again visited the literature for some possible clues, if not answers. It was interesting, he noted, that the "popular" writers, theorists and advocates were rarely directly connected with real change initiatives, at least not for any sustained period (Deal & Peterson, 1999; DuFour & Eaker, 1998; Fullan, 2001a). Most of this dialogue was based on brief one-time exposure to change efforts followed by some step-by-step formula approaches to change. Not that there weren't some lessons to be learned from that literature. Their models and constructs were usually wise and relevant; but they were fraught with difficulty if applied in a blanket "one-size-fits-all" manner. Instead Greg tried to focus on writers who had either experienced or studied leadership over a period of time (Elmore, 2000a; Leithwood, 1995; Leithwood & Jantzi, 2000). He gravitated toward Leithwood's transformational and Elmore's distributed models of leadership as frameworks for the future of leadership in Antelope Range. He felt that for the next phase of development to be successful:

- growth strategies had to be rooted in depth;
- "unlearning" many of the cultural traits would take time;
- the contextual factors in Antelope Range were central in developing responsive change; and
- school leaders needed to be skilled at creating a focused community effort to respond to students' learning needs.

Greg had brought the district into a new era. He had shaken people out of their complacency, and he had opened doors to new ways of learning, to professional growth and to accountability. His reflection focused on his change efforts and their varying degrees of success. Now he needed to build on these foundations and imagine what the school of the future would look like, and how Antelope Range would need to prepare for that type of school.* Next he had to instill the confidence, the commitment and the ownership into his district such that the changes would be embraced and empowering leadership would blossom.

Did he have enough years left to tackle this challenge?

---

*Leithwood (1999) thinks that schools of the future will evolve from today's schools on a broken front, over an unpredictable timeline. He also thinks that the changes will emerge in the form of marginal improvements, which will be quite different from the systemic change referred to throughout this text. "As much as we might wish that we are entering a brave new world in which many things (including schools) will somehow behave differently, the wisest bet is that incrementalism will prevail" (p. 219). Leithwood further states that there has been no evidence that radical change has occurred in the past – despite the rhetoric. A second reason for incremental change is that any change will require teacher and administrator learning – which is long-term and messy. On the other hand, he does support continuous improvement as a legitimate strategy with which to approach change in the school setting. "Continuous improvement is an antidote for the sense of being overwhelmed and confused that is fueled by excessively turbulent environments such as those currently faced by schools" (p. 222).

Workshop Questions:

1. To what extent is your school district cultivating change? Create a survey instrument that will gather data about analysis of achievement results, achievement targets and goals, focused research activity and responsive teacher growth plans.

2. How do you describe the learning culture in your school/district? What activity is highly valued in your school system? How do know what's valued? What are the measures to determine progress toward goals? To what extent are key stakeholders involved in contributing to the culture?

3. What are the barriers to attaining key goals in the district? Are the factors that prevent sustainable change easily identified, or do they lurk somewhere below the surface? How many of your staff willingly support a dialogue about teaching and learning?

4. Do an inventory of one school improvement initiative in your school/district.

References

Aitken, A., Gunderson, T. & Witchen, E. (2000). *AISI and the superintendent: Opportunities for new relationships.* Paper presented at the meeting of AISI Opportunities and Challenges, Edmonton, AB.

Alberta Education. (1995). *Roles and responsibilities in education: A position paper.* Edmonton, AB: Author.

Alberta Learning. (1998). *Accountability in education: Teacher growth, supervision and evaluation.* Edmonton, AB: Author.

Alberta Learning. (1999). *Professional development for teaching technology across the curriculum: Best practices for Alberta school jurisdictions.* Edmonton, AB: Author.

Ancess, J. (2000). The reciprocal influence of teacher learning, teaching practice, school restructuring, and student learning outcomes. *Teachers College Record, 102*(3), 590-619.

Bamburg, J. D. & Andrews, R. L. (1990, April). *Instructional leadership, school goals, and student achievement: Exploring the relationship between means and ends.* Paper presented at the meeting of the American Educational Research Association, Boston.

Barth, R. S. (2000). Learning to lead. In *Jossey-Bass reader on educational leadership* (pp. 146-155). San Francisco: Jossey-Bass.

Barth, R. S. (2001). *Learning by heart.* San Francisco: Jossey-Bass.

Blase, J. R. & Blase, J. (1998). *Handbook of instructional leadership: How really good principals promote teaching and learning.* Thousand Oaks, CA: Corwin Press.

Bolman, L. & Deal, T. (1997). *Reframing organizations: Artistry, choice, and leadership.* San Francisco: Jossey-Bass.

Bolman, L. & Deal, T. (2000a). The manager as politician. In *Jossey-Bass reader on educational leadership* (pp. 164-181). San Francisco: Jossey-Bass.

Bolman, L. & Deal, T. (2000b). People and organizations. In *Jossey-Bass reader on rducational leadership* (pp. 59-69). San Francisco: Jossey-Bass.

Brown, J. & Moffett, C. (1999). *The hero's journey: How educators can transform schools and improve learning.* Alexandria, VA: Association for Supervision and Curriculum Development.

Brubaker, D. L. & Coble, L. D. (1997). *Staying on track: An educational leader's guide to preventing derailment and ensuring personal and organizational success.* Thousand Oaks, CA: Corwin Press.

Burger, J., Aitken, A., Brandon, J., Klink, P., McKinnon, G. & Mutch, S. (2001). In pursuit of the next generation of basic education accountability in Alberta, Canada: A policy dialogue. *International Electronic Journal of Leadership in Learning, 5*(19). Retrieved from http://www.ucalgary.ca/iejll/2001./volume5.html

Caine, R. & Caine, G. (1994). *Making connections: Teaching and the human brain.* Alexandria: VA: Association for Supervision and Curriculum Development.

Caldwell, B. J. (2002). *Leadership and innovation in the transformation of schools.* Retrieved Dec. 11, 2002 from www.ncsl.org.uk/

Canadian Association of School Administrators. (1993). *Facing the realities: An agenda, process and leadership for reinventing schools and communities.* White Rock, BC: Canadian Association of School Administrators.

Carter, K. & Jackson, D. (2002). Introduction – leadership in urban and challenging contexts: Perspectives from the National College for School Leadership. *School Leadership & Management, 22*(1), 7-13.

Day, C., Harris, A., Hadfield, M., Tolley, H. & Beresford, J. (2000). *Leading schools in times of change.* Buckingham: Open University Press.

Deal, T. E. & Peterson, K. D. (1999). *Shaping school culture: The heart of leadership.* San Francisco: Jossey-Bass.

DuFour, R. & Eaker, R. (1998). *Professional learning communities at work: Best practices for enhancing student achievement.* Alexandria, VA: Association for Supervision and Curriculum Development.

Elmore, R. (2000a). *Building a new structure for school leadership.* Washington, DC: The Albert Shanker Institute.

Elmore, R. F. (2000b). Building a new structure for school leadership. *American Educator, 23*(4), 6-44.

Fullan, M. (1997). *The challenge of school change: A collection of articles.* Arlington Heights, IL: IRI/SkyLight Training and Publishing.

Fullan, M. (1999). *Change forces: The sequel.* London: Falmer Press.

Fullan, M. (2001a). *Leading in a culture of change.* San Francisco: Jossey-Bass.

Fullan, M. (2001b). *The new meaning of educational change* (3rd ed.). New York: Teachers College Press.

Gadamer, H. E. (1990). *Truth and method.* New York: Crossroad.

Gardner, H. (1991). *The unschooled mind: How children think and how schools should teach.* New York: Basic Books.

Guskey, T. R. (Ed.). (1996). *ASCD Year Book: Communicating student learning.* Alexandria, VA: Association for Supervision and Curriculum Development.

Hargreaves, D. (1998). *Creative professionalism: The role of teachers in the knowledge society.* London: Demos.

Heidegger, M. (1977). *Basic writings.* San Francisco: Harper.

Hord, S. M. (1994). The board's role in educational improvement. *Issues...About Change, 3*(4), 1-13.

Hord, S. M. (1997a). *Professional learning communities: Communities of continuous inquiry and improvement.* Retrieved January 18, 2003, from www.sedl.org/pubs/change34

Hord, S. M. (1997b). Professional learning communities: What are they and why are they important? *Issues... About Change, 6*(1), 1-8.

Jackson, D. (September 2000). *School improvement and the planned growth of leadership capacity.* Paper presented at the meeting of the BERA Conference, Cardiff, Wales.

Joyce, B., Calhoun, E. & Hopkins, D. (1999). *The new structure of school improvement: Inquiring schools and achieving students.* Buckingham: Open University Press.

Kagan, S. (1992). *Cooperative learning.* San Juan Capistrano, CA: Resources for Teachers, Inc.

Knight, P., Aitken, E. N. & Rogerson, R. J. (2000). *Forever better: Continuous quality improvement in higher education.* Stillwater, OK: New Forums Press.

Kouzes, J. M. & Posner, M. (2002). *Leadership challenge: How to keep getting extraordinary things done in organizations* (3rd ed.). San Francisco: Jossey-Bass.

Lambert, L. (1998). *Building leadership capacity in schools.* Alexandria, VA: Association for Supervision and Curriculum Development.

Leithwood, K. & Aitken, R. (1995). *Making schools smarter: A system for monitoring school and district progress.* Thousand Oaks, CA: Corwin Press.

Leithwood, K. A. & Jantzi, D. (2000). The effects of transformational leadership on organizational conditions and student engagement with school. *Journal of Educational Administration, 38*(2), 112-126.

Leithwood, K. A., Jantzi, D. & Steinbach, R. (1999). *Changing leadership for changing times.* Philadelphia: Open University Press.

Lieberman, A., Saxl, E. R. & Miles, M. B. (2000). Teacher leadership: Ideology and practice. In *Jossey-Bass reader on educational leadership* (pp. 348-366). San Francisco: Jossey-Bass.

Manzer, R. (1994). *Public schools and political ideas: Canadian educational policy in historical perspective.* Toronto, ON: University of Toronto Press.

Marsh, D. D. (2000). Educational leadership for the twenty-first century: Integrating three essential principles. In *Jossey-Bass reader on educational leadership* (pp. 126-145). San Francisco: Jossey-Bass.

Marzano, R. J., Pickering, D. & McTighe, J. (1993). *Assessing student outcomes: Performance assessment using the dimensions of learning model.* Alexandria, VA: Association for Supervision and Curriculum Development.

McAdams, R. P. & Zinck, R. A. (1998). The power of the superintendent's leadership in shaping school district culture: Three case studies. *ERS Spectrum, 16*(4), 3-7. (ERIC Document Reproduction Service EJ581467)

Moore Johnson, S. (2000). Looking for leaders. In *Jossey-Bass reader on educational leadership* (pp. 73-96). San Francisco: Jossey-Bass.

Murphy, J. & Louis, K. S. (1994). *Reshaping the principalship: Insights from transformational reform efforts.* Thousand Oaks, CA: Corwin Press.

Murphy, J. & National Society for the Study of Education. (2002). *The educational leadership challenge: Redefining leadership for the 21st century.* Chicago: University of Chicago Press.

Perkins, D. (1992). *Smart schools: From training memories to educating minds.* New York: Maxwell MacMillan Canada.

Peterson, K. D. & Deal, T. E. (2002). *The shaping school culture fieldbook.* San Francisco: Jossey-Bass.

Popham, W. J. (2000). *Modern educational measurement: Practical guidelines for educational leaders* (3rd ed.). Needham, MA: Allyn & Bacon.

Sandholtz, J. H., Ringstaff, C. & Dwyer, D. C. (1997). *Teaching with technology: Creating student-centered classrooms.* New York: Teachers College Press.

Saphier, J. & King, M. (1985). Good seeds grow in strong cultures. *Educational Leadership, 42*(6), 67-74.

Senge, P. (1994). *The fifth discipline field book: Strategies and tools for building a learning organization.* New York: Doubleday.

Senge, P. (1999). *The dance of change.* London: Routledge.

Sergiovanni, T. J. (2000). *The lifeworld of leadership: Creating culture, community, and personal meaning in our schools.* San Francisco: Jossey-Bass.

Slavin, R. E. (2003). A reader's guide to scientifically based research. *Educational Leadership, 60*(5), 12-16.

Slee, R. (2000). *The inclusive school.* New York: Falmer Press.

Smith, F. (1986). *Insult to intelligence: The bureaucratic invasion of our classrooms.* New York: Arbor House.

Sparks, D. & Hirsh, S. (1994). *A new vision for staff development.* Alexandria, VA: Association for Curriculum Development.

Spillane, J. P. & Seashore Louis, K. (2001). School improvement processes and practices: Professional learning for building instructional capacity. In J. Murphy (Ed.), *The educational leadership challenge: Redefining leadership for the 21st century* (pp. 83-104). Chicago, IL: The National Society for the Study of Education.

van Manen, M. (1990). *Researching lived experience: Human science for an action sensitive pedagogy* ON: Althouse Press.

Wheatley, M. (2000). Good-bye, command and control. In *Jossey-Bass reader on educational leadership* (pp. 339-347). San Francisco: Jossey-Bass.

Willis, S. (1996). On the cutting edge of assessment: Testing what students can do with knowledge. *Education Update, Association for Supervision and Curriculum Development, 38*(4), 1, 4-7.

Related Readings

Begley, P. T. & Leonard, P. E. (Eds.). (1999). *The values of educational administration*. New York: Falmer Press.

Brandt, R. S. (Ed.). (2000). *Education in a new era. ASCD Year Book 2000*. Alexandria, VA: Association for Supervision and Curriculum Development.

DePree, M. (1997). *Leading without power: Finding hope in serving community*. San Francisco, Jossey-Bass.

Evans, R. (2000). The authentic leader. In Jossey-Bass Education Series, *Educational leadership* (pp. 287-308). San Francisco: Jossey-Bass.

Hamilton, D. & Zaretsky, L. (1997). Building professional communities of inquiry in schools, *Orbit, 28*(3), 44-47.

Hargreaves, A. (Ed.). (1997). *Rethinking educational change with heart and mind. 1997 ASCD Year Book*. Alexandria, VA: Association for Supervision and Curriculum Development.

Jensen, E. (1998). *Teaching with the brain in mind*. Reston, VA: Association for Supervision and Curriculum Development.

Jossey-Bass Education Series. (2000). *Educational leadership*. San Francisco: Jossey Bass Inc., Publishers.

Leithwood, K. (Ed.). (1995). *Effective school district leadership: Transforming politics into education*. Albany, NY: State University of New York Press.

Murphy, J. (1992). *The landscape of leadership preparation: Reframing the education of school administrators*. Newbury Park, CA: Corwin Press.

Patterson, J. L. (1993). *Leadership for tomorrow's schools*. Alexandria, VA: Association for Supervision and Curriculum Development.

Sergiovanni, T. J. (1992). *Moral leadership: Getting to the heart of school improvement*. San Francisco: Jossey-Bass Inc., Publishers.

Sergiovanni, T. J. (1996). *Leadership for the schoolhouse: How is it different? Why is it important?* San Francisco: Jossey-Bass Inc., Publishers.

Short, P. M. & Greer, J. T. (1997). *Leadership in empowered schools: Themes from innovative efforts*. Upper Saddle River, NJ: Merrill.

Sinclair, A. (1998). *Doing leadership differently: Gender, power, and sexuality in a changing business culture*. Melbourne, Victoria, Australia: Melbourne University Press.

Developing the Antelope Range Beliefs Statement

Draft Statement	Final Statement (modifications in italics)
Every student is capable of learning.	Every *person* is capable of learning.
Learners respect each other.	Every *person respects the dignity* of others.
Home and school share responsibility for student learning.	*Home and community play a vital role* in the learning process.
Effective teachers facilitate learning.	The *learner-teacher relationship* is the core to the school experience.
Engaged learning requires active participation in a risk-free environment.	Learning is an engaging activity that is negotiated in a *safe and secure* environment.
	Education, which encompasses the process of learning, is a shared responsibility.
Every person in our system learns in a unique way.	Every person in our system *is valued* and learns in a unique way.
Schools are accountable for results.	Accountability to student learning is *the core business at all levels of school system* operations.
Success in learning is dependent upon selecting an appropriate approach for each child and a focus on the whole child.	Success in learning is accomplished by *balancing academic achievement with an appropriate emphasis on the emotional, physical, creative and social development of the student.*

Antelope Range Leadership Capacity Staff Survey (adapted)

This is an assessment of leadership dispositions, knowledge and skills needed to build leadership capacity in Antelope Range schools. Principals can ask staff to participate such that the instrument could be used for reflection and dialogue. The survey is most useful if used as a self-assessment instrument.

    1 = Doesn't happen

    2 = Infrequently performed

    3 = Frequently

    4 = Consistently performed

    5 = Exemplary practice

Please circle the appropriate response.

A. Broad-based participation in leadership. **In our school, the teacher...**

	1	2	3	4	5
1. Assists in the governance of the school (committees).					
2. Maximizes interactions among all school and community members.					
3. Shares authority and resources broadly.					
4. Promotes opportunities for others to lead.					

TOTALS

B. Skillful participation in the work of leadership. **In our school, the teacher...**

	1	2	3	4	5
5. Models, describes and demonstrates by:					
a. developing shared purpose and meaning of learning					
b. facilitating group processes					
c. communicating (listening and questioning)					
d. reflecting on practice					
e. inquiring into school community issues					
f. collaborating in planning					
g. managing adult conflicts					
h. problem-solving with others					
i. managing resources					
j. using constructivist learning designs					
6. Communicates through action and words the connection between leadership and learning.					

TOTALS

C. Inquiry-based use of information to inform shared decisions and practice. **In our school, the teacher...**

	1	2	3	4	5
7. Engages with others in a purposeful reflection and dialogue					
8. Identifies, discovers and interprets information and school data/evidence					
9. Designs and implements a way of sharing the data					
10. Participates in a process to integrate the data into decision-making.					

TOTALS

D. Roles and responsibilities that reflect broad involvement and collaboration. **In our school, the teacher...**

	1	2	3	4	5
11. Pays attention to classroom, the school, the community, and the profession					
12. Observes and encourages innovations					
13. Encourages new relationships based on collaboration					
14. Develops strategies to implement school-community agreements.					

TOTALS

E. Reflective practice/innovation as the norm. **In our school, the teacher...**

	1	2	3	4	5
15. Volunteers continuous reflective opportunities					
16. Supports initiatives by providing resources					
17. Supports innovations by allowing time for development					
18. Participates in collaborative innovation					
19. Collectively develops rubrics for evaluating individual and shared work.					

TOTALS

F. High student achievement. **In our school, the teacher...**

	1	2	3	4	5
20. Works collectively to establish challenging standards					
21. Encourages use of authentic and performance-based assessment processes					
22. Provides meaningful feedback to learners					
23. Consults families regarding expectations					
24. Encourages responsible, not dependent, learning					
25. Encourages practices that include inquiry and reflection on results.					

TOTALS

Rubrics for Teacher Evaluation

The concept of student involvement in rubrics was applied to Antelope Range for the Evaluation of Teachers with Interim Certification (beginning teachers) and Permanent Certification. Input was gathered from interest groups such as principals, the ATA and teachers themselves, and reworked until it reached an acceptable point. The collaborative process was challenging and marked with some resistance, but the final product was accepted as a tool to assist in the teacher evaluation process and was also intended as a reflective tool for interested practitioners.

First, however, some background on rubrics. A rubric is a vehicle used to guide human judgment. Its origin is from the Latin rubrica terra that refers to "the use of red earth centuries ago to mark or signify something of importance" (Marzano, Pickering & McTighe, 1993, p. 29). Another name for rubric is "scoring guide." The spirit of the original meaning of rubric is used today, since the term commonly means an authoritative or established rule. Specifically it consists of a fixed scale of values or characteristics along with performance levels describing the characteristics. There are two kinds of rubrics in use, holistic, and analytic.

A holistic rubric views performance and product responses as a whole and the evaluator gives the response and overall grade. A well-constructed holistic rubric can come up with high interrater reliability, (high interjudgment agreements means that when different judges score the same essays they produce remarkably consistent scores) (Guskey, 1996; Popham, 2000). Holistic scoring is faster and comparisons are easier to make. The weakness, however, is that it is not so helpful in providing people with detailed feedback. Because holistic rubrics provide globalized and not particularized feedback of strengths and weaknesses, it makes it difficult for learners to identify which specific areas need to be improved.

Analytic scoring, on the other hand, provides more diagnostic information; it requires that people know during the instructional process what is expected of them on prespecified dimensions of their work. It requires sufficient information on each criterion for judgments to be made reliably, and it enables a performance or product to be judged on multiple criteria (summary scores may reveal that two performances achieve equal ratings, but are very different from one another). It is much easier to pinpoint the strengths and weaknesses of a performance or product when using an analytic rubric because each criterion and level that has been achieved is exposed so that the person can address his or her areas of strength and weakness. This is the advantage it has over the holistic rubric where just the overall picture is presented (Guskey, 1996; Popham, 2000).

"Student-constructed rubrics" are those where the student and teacher together construct the rubric for a task or product. Danielson (Willis, 1996) believes that students involved with developing their rubrics for performance tasks will more likely hit the target, in that they understand what they are supposed to do.

> "…it helps enormously to involve students in developing rubrics which help spell out the criteria for different levels of performance," Danielson says. "In the past, the assessment process has been kind of mysterious,' she contends; students were 'shooting blind.' But when students are involved in developing assessment criteria, 'the kids know what they have to do to [perform] well – and guess what? They do it.'" (Willis, 1996, p. 4)

Jointly constructed rubrics work equally well with adults who are involved in setting clear performance targets for agreed-upon teaching standards. When teachers have input into policy and performance standards, they understand the purposes and criteria better, and consequently have more "buy in."

The teacher evaluation rubric for beginning teachers follows in Figure C1.

Figure C1. Rubrics for the evaluation of teachers with Interim Certification (beginning teachers)

Teaching domains are indicated by Roman numeral headings (I, … V)

Teaching standards are indicated with upper case letters (A, B, C, etc.), and reflect the standards specified in the Ministerial Order.

The rubric can be interpreted as

4 - superior teaching

3 - meeting the standard

2 - needs some improvement

1 - not acceptable (requires an immediate improvement plan)

I. Planning for Learning

A. The teacher understands that contextual variables affect teaching and learning:

4 The teacher insightfully analyses most relevant contextual variables to make meaningful effective decisions about her/his teaching practice and student learning.

3 The teacher knows how to analyze many variables at one time, and how to respond by making reasoned decisions about her/his teaching practice and students' learning.

2 The teacher recognizes some variables but fails to analyze them or only superficially does so, such that teaching practices and students' learning remains largely decontextualized.

1 The teacher either fails to acknowledge all but the most obvious contextual variables, or in-appropriately analyzes variables to inform teaching practices and student learning.

B. The teacher understands the purposes of the Guide to Education and Programs of Study germane to the specialization or subject disciplines he/she is prepared to teach:

4 The teacher insightfully interprets and reflects an enhanced understanding of curriculum documents in teaching preparation and practice. Supplementary resources are skillfully used to enhance learning.

3 The teacher uses curriculum documents to inform and direct her/his planning, instructing and assessing student progress. Use of supplementary resources is aligned with curriculum topics.

2 The teacher's planning and teaching practice only partially reflects content of curriculum documents. Teaching decisions reflect an over dependence upon text and commercial resources.

1 The teacher either has no knowledge of curriculum documents or fails to implement content to inform teaching. Teaching decisions are severely restricted because of dependence on worksheets, textbooks or computer software, which may minimally comply with expected outcomes expressed in curriculum documents.

C. The teacher understands the subject disciplines he/she teaches:

4 The teacher demonstrates an in-depth understanding of the subject disciplines being taught. The teacher's insightful interpretation of the content area is reflected in planning, assessment and instructional pedagogy.

3 The teacher's practice is informed by the knowledge, concepts, methodologies and assumptions from one or more curriculums of specialization or subject disciplines taught in the province's schools. Pedagogy is consistent with the expected learner outcomes.

2 Teaching reflects a partial understanding of the subject discipline. Planning and methodology lack a systematic translation of the subject discipline and understanding of key concepts is at a superficial level.

1 The teacher demonstrates little or no understanding of content area. Teaching is characterized by either misinterpretation of the subject discipline or is marked by omission of important concepts.

D. The teacher understands the purpose of short, medium and long range planning:

4 The teacher's planning reflects a design that supports and recognizes the general expected outcomes, outlines a balance and variety of connected learning activities, accommodates atypical learners and includes appropriate assessment practices. Timing, sequencing and flexibility are acknowledged and skillfully incorporated.

3 The teacher knows how to translate curriculum and desired outcomes into reasoned, meaningful and incrementally progressive learning opportunities for all students. Planning reflects an appropriate sequence of topics.

2 The teacher's planning only superficially addresses concept development but lack of detail invites problems in sequencing, aligning, assessment and organizing meaningful learning activities. Planning is sometimes an unconnected exercise to respond to requirements and fails to link closely with teaching.

1 The teacher's planning is either non-existent, a mirror image of text topics, or insufficient to assist the teaching/learning process in any meaningful way. Teaching becomes either a series of disjointed activities or it is completely dependent on text content.

II. Facilitates Learning

A. The teacher understands that all students can learn, albeit at different rates and in different ways.

4 The teacher works collaboratively to accurately identify students' different learning styles and approaches to learning. All students are provided with divergent learning opportunities that capitalize upon their strengths and accommodate differences.

3 The teacher knows how to identify students' different learning styles, developmental needs and ways students learn. The teaching reflects a response to differences by creating multiple paths to learning for individuals and groups of students, including students with special learning needs.

2 The teacher remains largely dependent upon his/her dominant learning style, instructing the class in essentially unidimensional paths to learning for most students. The teacher attempts to address the most apparent learning needs.

1 The teacher is unaware of learning styles and instructs all students irrespective of learning needs.

B. The teacher understands that there are many approaches to teaching and learning:

4 The teacher consistently employs a broad range of instructional strategies appropriate to her/his area of specialization and the subject disciplines he/she teaches, and he/she insightfully selects appropriate strategies and outcomes that maximize learning for most students.

3 The teacher knows a broad range of instructional strategies appropriate to her/his area of specialization and the subject discipline he/she teaches, and knows which strategies are appropriate to help different students achieve different outcomes.

2 The teacher is familiar with a few instructional strategies appropriate to his/her subject discipline but is unable to discern the strategy most appropriate to the particular outcome or student being instructed.

1 The teacher relies upon a dominant instructional strategy irrespective of the subject discipline being taught, the outcome intended or the particular student being instructed.

C. The teacher understands the functions of traditional and electronic teaching/learning technologies:

4 The teacher and students explore and utilize a range of relevant traditional and electronic teaching/learning technologies to enhance the way they deliver and present content, communicate with others, find and secure information, research, word process, manage information and keep records.

3 The teacher knows how to use, and how to engage students in using, traditional electronic learning technologies to present and deliver content, communicate effectively with others, find and secure information, research, word process, manage information and keep records.

2 The teacher has a limited ability to use technologies and provides students with limited opportunities to use them for research, word processing, managing information and keeping records.

1 The teacher does not use technology and fails to engage students in its use or does so inappropriately.

D. The teacher understands the importance of engaging parents, purposefully and meaningfully, in all aspects of teaching and learning:

4 The teacher fosters the development of effective partnerships among teacher, parents and students that improve learning opportunities for students.

3 The teacher knows how to develop and implement strategies that create and enhance partnerships among teachers, parents and students.

2 The teacher is aware of the benefits of partnerships among teachers, parents and students but has difficulty implementing the strategies necessary to develop them.

1 The teacher is unaware of the benefits or uncommitted to the development of learning partnerships among parents, teachers and students.

E. The teacher understands that student learning is enhanced through the use of home and community resources:

4 The teacher and students identify and capitalize on a variety of home and community resources relevant to the teaching and learning objectives such that both teaching and learning are meaningfully enhanced.

3 The teacher identifies home and community resources relevant to teaching and learning objectives, and incorporates these resources into teaching and students' learning.

2 The teacher identifies only obvious links to home and community resources but either under-utilizes or fails to utilize them.

1 The teacher is largely unaware of links to home and community resources and fails to mention or utilize any.

III. Assessing and Evaluating Learning:

A. The teacher understands the purposes of student assessment:

4 Assessment practices are fair, balanced and purposefully aligned with general expected outcomes with a view to improving learning. A variety of assessments provide students with opportunities to demonstrate what they know. Assessment is an integral part of planning, it supports evaluation and it drives purposeful teaching.

3 The teacher knows how to assess the range of learning objectives by selecting and developing a variety of classroom and large-scale assessment techniques and instruments. Teacher-made tools form the basis of assessment practice. The teacher analyzes the results of classroom and large-scale assessment, including provincial assessment results, with a view to student benefit.

2 Assessment practices are limited to 'unit tests' and use of large-scale instruments. Testing is usually designed to collect comparative data and to be translated to marks. Focus is often on mistakes, and opportunities to learn often go wanting.

1 Assessment practices are insufficient to draw any meaningful evaluation of student learning. Tests are usually limited to commercial test material. Tests that are teacher designed are often unfair, not based on lesson content.

IV. Classroom Management

A. The teacher understands students' needs for physical, social, cultural and psychological security:

4 The teacher's concern for security is sincere, consistent and pervasive. The teacher carefully orchestrates a safe and secure learning environment. The learning atmosphere is supported and enhanced by creating and sustaining meaningful routines, mutual respect and individual credibility.

3 Security and safety is acknowledged and stressed. The teacher knows how to engage students in creating effective classroom routines. He/she knows how and when to apply a variety of management strategies that are in keeping with the situation and that provide for minimal disruptions to students' learning.

2 Student well-being is often marginalized. Classroom routines are sporadic and inconsistently applied. Management strategies are often used to challenge students, frequently resulting in conflict issues, disrupting the learning environment on a re-occurring basis.

1 Student safety is neglected. Classroom routines are either non-existent or totally ineffective. Management strategies are limited, resulting in disruptive conflict issues. Discipline issues seriously impede meaningful learning.

B. The teacher understands the importance of respecting students' human dignity:

4 The teacher actively engages in and models relationships that are built on acceptance, understanding and mutual respect. Students respond positively to routines, strategies and communication that foster successful interpersonal relations.

3 The teacher knows how to establish, with different students, professional relationships that are characterized by mutual respect, trust and harmony. Students respond positively to classroom routines.

2 The teacher attempts to promote — but frequently demands – respect from the students. Not all students are treated consistently, and standards of conduct are confusing.

1 Relationships are marred by disrespect and disregard for human dignity. Student learning is jeopardized by a dysfunctional interpersonal structure.

V. Professional Qualities

A. The teacher understands the structure of the provincial education system:

4 The teacher consistently supports and demonstrates an understanding of the different roles in the system, and how responsibilities and accountabilities are determined, communicated and enforced, including the expectations held of her/him under the *Certification of Teachers Regulation*; and the school authority's teacher evaluation policy.

3 The teacher knows the different roles in the system, and how responsibilities and accountabilities are determined, communicated and enforced, including the expectations held of her/him under the *Certification of Teachers Regulation*; and the school authority's teacher evaluation policy.

2 The teacher is unsure of the different roles in the system, and how responsibilities and accountabilities are determined, communicated and enforced, including the expectations held of her/him under the *Certification of Teachers Regulation*; and the school authority's teacher evaluation policy.

1 The teacher shows disregard, and frequently disrespect, for the different roles in the system, and how responsibilities and accountabilities are determined, communicated and enforced, including the expectations held of her/him under the *Certification of Teachers Regulation*; and the school authority's teacher evaluation policy.

B. The teacher understands the importance of contributing, independently and collegially, to the quality of his/her school:

4 The teacher regularly and insightfully selects and employs strategies that independently and collegially enhance the quality of her/his school to the benefit of students, parents, community and colleagues.

3 The teacher uses strategies whereby he/she can, independently and collegially, enhance and maintain the quality of her/his school to the benefit of students, parents, community and colleagues.

2 The teacher infrequently uses practices to enhance and maintain the quality of her/his school to the benefit of students, parents, community and colleagues, and he/she only marginally contributes to the quality of the school.

1 The teacher fails to use strategies whereby he/she can enhance and maintain the quality of her/his school to the benefit of students, parents, community and colleagues, and often undermines participation in quality building-activity.

C. The teacher understands the importance of career-long learning:

4 The teacher regularly engages in successful assessment of her/his own teaching and works collaboratively with others responsible for supervising and evaluating teachers. He/she insightfully selects, develops, and implements her/his own PD activities.

3 The teacher assesses her/his own teaching and works with others responsible for supervising and evaluating teachers. He/she knows how to use the findings of assessments, supervision and evaluations to select, develop and implement her/his own professional development activities.

2 The teacher is aware of self-assessment practices but fails to utilize the findings of such assessment to inform professional growth. He/she cooperates reluctantly with supervision and evaluation directives.

1 The teacher is unaware of or incapable of self-assessment practices that inform teacher professional growth. He/she disregards or resists supervision and evaluation directives.

D. The teacher understands the importance of guiding his/her actions with a personal, overall vision of the purpose of teaching:

4 The teacher models her/his vision about teaching and learning, and demonstrates how it evolves as a result of new knowledge, understanding and experiences.

3 The teacher is able to communicate his/her vision, including how it informed by new knowledge, understanding and experience.

2 The teacher is unclear about her/his vision and is unsure about how to incorporate new knowledge, understanding and experience.

1 The teacher's vision about teaching and learning is either inflexible, counter productive or nonexistent.

Antelope Range District #99

Classroom Innovation Program
Project Application

Name:

The proposal clearly focuses on enhanced pedagogical practices such that learners will be engaged using appropriate technologies, and responsible learning in a sustainable culture.

The following guidelines are intended to assist teachers in preparing proposals for funding under the ARD Classroom Innovation Program.

Selection for funding will be based upon the following criteria:

1. The proposal clearly links the technologies to a range of core curricular and Information and Communication Technology specific learner outcomes.

2. The proposal identifies the ongoing teaching, learning methods and activities that are supported by the technologies.

3. The proposal identifies adequate levels of current teacher competence with the technology and identifies ongoing professional growth and skill development.

4. The proposal shows evidence of using additional funding sources.

5. Relevant assessment of student learning and project success is clearly identified.

6. The proposal contains evidence of support from the school community: administration, parents.

7. The teacher will employ reflective practice techniques to link relevant theory to classroom learning. The following foci are encouraged:

   ● Multiple intelligences
   ● Cooperative learning
   ● Brain based research: implications for teaching and learning
   ● Enquiry-based learning
   ● Authentic assessment
   ● Teaching critical thinking skills
   ● Student centered instruction
   ● Multi-aging
   ● Inclusion practices
   ● Project approach to curriculum

Use these cues to help you respond to the above criteria:

1. Curricular Links

How do you propose to infuse ICT outcomes into core curriculum? (i.e., Projects, Web Quests, Web Explorations, Multimedia, Spreadsheets, Databases)

How do the projects develop a deeper understanding of expected outcomes?

What ICT outcomes are you targeting in this proposal? (Include the outcome and the strand)

2. Teaching and Learning Methods

Teaching strategies (i.e., Cooperative Learning, Flex Scheduling, Project-based learning, direct instruction, etc...)

Teaching and learning processes as a result of integrating technology seamlessly into the learning environment (include organization, structure, activities, etc.)

Typical schedule, teacher's role, student responsibilities

How will you reflect upon your teaching practice throughout the year? How will you be prepared to share this with other mentoring teachers and staff in your school?

3. Teacher Professional Growth and Development

ARD Teacher Technology Competency Skill List

Professional Development/Training Required

4. Funding

2Learn

School Council

5. Assessment

How will you evaluate and report the success or failure of your project?

How will you share your experiences with your colleagues and community?

How will students demonstrate their learning (process/product)?

How will you assess student achievement?

6. School Community Support

A letter of support from your administrator

Presentation to parent council outlining proposals

Frequently Asked Questions

Frequently Asked Questions provide quick responses to common questions that arise in the administrator's daily work. These can also be used as scenarios for leadership workshops where the participants can be grouped into "schools" and come up with "answers." After the responses are shared with the large group, the "expert" opinion cited can be used and debated. Another way of doing this is to get maximum involvement with large groups is by using a "Pairs Share" (Kagan, 1992). Each pair comes up with the solution and then turns to the adjacent pair and both pairs take turns to share. This new group of 4 can then turn to another resulting group of four and repeat the process, coming up with a streamlined solution for each question.

Question 1

"Overall I have a pretty good staff, but as in any box of apples, I have a few teachers who are resisting positive change and innovation. I want to keep up the good staff morale and camaraderie, but these few resisters to change are beginning to give me (and I suspect others) a sour taste. My question is, how do you deal with resisters effectively?"

The Aitken Answer:

"Don't vilify the resisters! If you do so, your respect quotient will start to wane. Engage them in a dialogue. Seek first to understand. Openly acknowledge the resistance in a positive way. If the debate is around authentic issues, then embrace it and seek resolution. But, don't privilege the resistance by providing too much airtime for the perpetrators. Having said all of that, you need to be prepared to move on at some point and not get bogged down. Acknowledge perhaps that 100% agreement and conformity are not possible, continue to provide support for those willing to make the change, and ensure that resisters are not taking a destructive path. If you encounter behavior that will derail the initiative, then you must go into conflict-resolution mode!"

Question 2

"What is some advice for new principals making changes in their school? I've heard that it is a good idea to go with the status quo for the first year, but then others have said, 'make hay while the sun shines during the honeymoon period.'"

The Aitken Answer:

"It depends a great deal on the context with respect to students, teachers and community. Identify the important data quickly but thoroughly and set out a course of action. Depending on the context, you might want to go slowly at first. It is important to establish fundamental management practice in your school and to ensure that the support services are focused and efficient. Work quietly on developing working relationships with staff, while at the same time engage staff in a dialogue that will inform you about the teaching practices and standards in the school. Make sure that your first initiatives are doable and carry a relatively high profile. Start conversations about goals, plans and learning needs. Use staff meetings, school council meetings and the media to state your intentions to do a needs assessment and to begin work on creating (or building on) a learning culture that values student achievement and quality teaching practice. That might be enough for the first year, but finish the year with a definite plan that will set the agenda for your second year in the position."

Question 3

"I'm a principal in a small school district who actually is onside with the superintendent who is focusing on improving teaching and learning in the schools. I'm being seen as having other motives by my fellow principals and feeling some isolation. What advice do you have for me?"

The Aitken Answer:

"If your 'other motives' are positive, student focused and even career oriented you are on safe ground. However, if you are seen to be sacrificing your integrity and violating standards simply to 'align yourself' with the superintendent, then you are going to have a tough time maintaining positive working relationships with your peers. My suggestion is to reflect on your purposes and your strategies. Take the high ground on principles, values and learning matters. Be careful not to burn your bridges with colleagues but model your standards and your loyalties and you will earn the respect of those people who count!"

Question 4

"I'm in a dilemma with two factions of parents who sit on opposite sides of the fence when it comes to teaching and learning. For example, one group has very traditional thinking about learning, while the other is progressive. I know I have work to do to bring the sides together but I don't know where to start. The sniping between the two groups is starting to affect the Parent Council Meetings in a negative way. How should I begin to address this without being unpopular with one group?"

The Aitken Answer:

"Encourage the debate in a pro-active manner. Stand behind the role of the professional. Ask your teachers to make presentations to school council about the pedagogical practice in your school. We can acknowledge that in some cases there are no right answers and in other cases, student learning needs will inform us of the appropriate practice. Encourage enquiry. You might be able to encourage parents to form a study group (with your teachers?) to research the opposing views and report back to council. Bottom line, the professional decisions about learning will be made by the professionals based on current understanding of the context."

Question 5

"I have two energetic and forward thinking and effective teachers on staff. They are popular with parents and students but I can see that this is resulting in some jealousy from the rest of the staff who are suspicious about their teaching styles and approaches. I have asked them to do some PD at staff meetings, but it was not well-received in spite of an excellent work-

shop that was purposeful, relevant and well-executed. Now what?"

The Aitken Answer:

"Reflective practice and purposeful dialogue need to be skillfully orchestrated. If you are promoting a change in culture that supports risk, innovation and informed pedagogical practice, then it will take time. Be persistent and consistent. Create the 'beliefs about learning discussion' and encourage research, risk and sharing of ideas. The momentum will pick up if you tout the virtues of a professional learning community. Do not abide disrespect and unprofessional behavior."

Question 6

"My teachers and support staff are interested in participating in professional development programs. But these programs do not align with the grants and funds that are allocated by the board for designated growth and development initiatives. How can I reconcile this dilemma in a school budget that has limited resources?"

The Aitken Answer:

"You cannot reconcile this one if you have school goals and teacher growth goals that are independent of system directions and vision. Clearly you will need to use your own school funds if you choose to support this activity. The answer lies in taking an active role in developing system goals. But once these goals are established, you need as a principal to model and represent the system directions and encourage your staff to do so as well."

Question 7

"A few of my staff members have adopted the use of technology to support some components of their teaching. However, the majority of my staff lack the confidence, interest or disposition to effectively use technology. How can I implement a provincially-mandated curriculum in the face of these limited resources?"

Aitken Answer:

"You can't. You have to continue to encourage your staff to learn more about the virtues and relevance of meaningful technology. We need to continue with an ongoing dialogue with our community about the curriculum and staff efforts to give students the opportunities to function well in the 21st century. The reality of technology is such that your teachers need to be prepared to use and think of it as one of the basic forms of literacy."

Question 8

"My staff and many of my parents complain that I'm not accessible because I'm constantly out of the school attending meetings. How can I meet my systemic obligations and at the same time meet my obligations to communicate effectively at the school level?"

Aitken Answer:

"This is a tough one! But as much as possible you need to control your own agenda. Identify your priorities and the type of activities that will take you out of your building and review these with your staff and community. The balancing act requires that you develop an understanding of what it takes for your school to be an effective partner within the larger community. Don't forget the absences from your school create an opportunity for empowerment and shared leadership."

Question 9

"Our board has set a goal to enhance our profile in the community. Many of the staff are uncomfortable and stressed with the consequent ongoing exposure to the media. Some claim it's a 3-ring circus. How can I attend to this goal without further exacerbating the pressure on my staff?"

The Aitken Answer:

"The answer lies in how you approach and adopt strategies to meet system goals. Clearly if you involve your staff in formulating those strategies you will have a better buy in and you'll be more likely at least to achieve some level of satisfactory results, such as fewer intrusions and more meaningful publicity. This will have to be a cooperative effort that requires some skillful negotiation. The media, the teachers and the administration will have to make some concessions in search of a workable plan."

Question 10

"My staff is tired of talking. The constant demands for input, site decisions, reflective discussions and dialogue about teaching pedagogy are taking the focus away from the classroom. Why can't we just close our doors and do our jobs?"

The Aitken Answer:

"You could – if this was the 1950s."

Index

accountability, 7, 11, 16, 18, 24, 27, 28, 30, 33, 40, 46, 47, 49, 50, 53, 54, 55, 57, 63, 67, 68, 69, 70, 79, 88

action research, 11, 51

"adopters, adapters & resisters", 11, 39, 42, 68

beliefs, 10, 23, 24, 25, 26, 27, 28, 29, 31, 34, 38, 40, 47, 54, 68, 79, 94

change, 11, 26, 61, 69, 70, 71, 93

collaborative approaches, 9, 29, 30, 31, 32, 47, 48, 55, 83

communication, 18

culture, 11, 16, 23, 24, 26, 29, 30, 32, 46, 57, 61, 63, 64, 65, 68, 69, 70, 91

funding, 11, 46, 50, 62, 65, 91

governance, 7, 9, 15, 16, 17, 18, 24, 27, 63, 69, 81

job-embedded practice, 11, 51

language, 11, 23, 29, 47, 48, 62

leadership:
    development, 9, 31, 32, 33, 93
    facilitative, 32,
    qualities of, 31, 48, 57, 70, 81, 82
    school/district, 16, 17, 23, 24, 26, 27, 29, 30, 34, 37, 39, 40, 47, 53, 54, 61, 67, 69
    shared, 40, 41

learning community, 9, 23, 24, 25, 26, 27, 29, 30, 31, 32, 33, 34, 41, 42, 45, 50, 53, 68

media (journalists), 15, 20, 95

modeling practices, 30, 40, 48, 49, 50, 68, 81, 87, 89, 94

peer coaching (mentoring), 11, 51, 68, 92

principal evaluation, 57

reflective practice, 10, 19, 24, 32, 48, 67, 82, 83, 91, 92, 94, 95

resistance, 11, 24, 29, 37, 39, 68, 83, 93

rubrics, 12, 32, 47, 48, 49, 82, 83-89

school improvement, 7, 21, 26, 29, 61, 62, 71

shared decision-making, 10, 21, 31, 40, 53, 69

site-based decision making (SBDM), 7, 17, 18, 19, 21, 23, 24, 30, 31, 40, 46, 54, 69, 95

small schools, 9, 11, 61-65, 67

study groups, 11, 51

teaching:
    effectiveness, 25, 26, 27, 38, 45, 51
    evaluation, 11, 26, 31, 45, 46, 48, 54, 83, 84-89
    pedagogy, 23, 29, 68, 95
    professional development, 11, 34, 40, 41, 45, 46, 50, 51, 53, 56, 68, 69, 70, 71, 84
    professionalization of teachers, 7, 9-10, 27, 40, 53, 57
    standards, 11, 26, 32, 37, 50, 84

technology (implementation in classrooms), 7, 11, 24, 26, 32, 37-42, 49, 53, 56, 57, 62, 67, 68, 69, 91, 92, 94, 95

Reader's Notes

Reader's Notes

Reader's Notes

Reader's Notes

Reader's Notes